BEING
OF
POWER

ALSO BY BARON BAPTISTE

Books/Kit

Change Your Body and Awaken the Sacred Within Your Soul

Journey Into Power: How to Sculpt Your Ideal Body, Free Your True Self, and Transform Your Life with Yoga

My Daddy Is a Pretzel: Yoga for Parents and Kids (illustrations by Sophie Fatus)

The Yoga Bootcamp Box: An Interactive Program to Revolutionize Your Life with Yoga (Kit)

DVDs

Baron Baptiste: Foundations of Power Vinyasa Yoga, Live at the San Francisco Conference

Baron Baptiste Live!: Core Power

Baron Baptiste Live!: Soul of Strength

Baron Baptiste Live!: Unlocking Athletic Power

Baron Baptiste's Power Yoga Level 1: The Initial Challenge

Baron Baptiste's Power Yoga Level 2: The Next Challenge

Baron Baptiste's Power Yoga Level 3: The Ultimate Challenge

Journey Into Power: Power Vinyasa Yoga, Level 1

Journey Into Power: Power Vinyasa Yoga, Level 2

The Trainer's Edge: Long and Lean Yoga

Transform Your Life: Yoga with Baron Baptiste

Please visit:

Hay House USA: **www.hayhouse.com**®
Hay House Australia: **www.hayhouse.com.au**
Hay House UK: **www.hayhouse.co.uk**
Hay House South Africa: **www.hayhouse.co.za**
Hay House India: **www.hayhouse.co.in**

BEING OF POWER

THE 9 PRACTICES TO IGNITE AN EMPOWERED LIFE

BARON BAPTISTE

HAY HOUSE, INC.
Carlsbad, California • New York City
London • Sydney • Johannesburg
Vancouver • Hong Kong • New Delhi

Published and distributed in the United States by: Hay House, Inc.: www.hayhouse.com® • *Published and distributed in Australia by:* Hay House Australia Pty. Ltd.: www.hayhouse.com.au • *Published and distributed in the United Kingdom by:* Hay House UK, Ltd.: www.hayhouse.co.uk • *Published and distributed in the Republic of South Africa by:* Hay House SA (Pty), Ltd.: www.hayhouse.co.za • *Distributed in Canada by:* Raincoast: www.raincoast.com • *Published in India by:* Hay House Publishers India: www.hayhouse.co.in

Cover design: Rodrigo Corral • Interior design: Nick C. Welch

Library of Congress Cataloging-in-Publication Data

Baptiste, Baron.
  Being of power : the nine practices to ignite an empowered life / Baron Baptiste. -- 1st ed.
    p. cm.
  ISBN 978-1-4019-1905-4 (hbk. : alk. paper) 1. Self-realization. 2. Conduct of life. 3. Yoga--Philosophy. I. Title.
  BJ1470.B37 2013
  158.1--dc23
                                    2012033301

ISBN: 978-1-4019-1905-4
Digital ISBN: 978-1-4019-3191-9

16 15 14 13   5 4 3 2
1st edition, April 2013
2nd edition, April 2013

SUSTAINABLE
FORESTRY
INITIATIVE
Certified Chain of Custody
Promoting Sustainable Forestry
www.sfiprogram.org
SFI-01268
SFI label applies to the text stock

Printed in the United States of America

To Luke, Jake, and Malachi, all on their way to creating a life that matters. . . . And to Mom, who at 91 years continues to live an extraordinary life that inspires.

CONTENTS

INTRODUCTION

In 1926, Albert Einstein told his fellow physicist Werner Heisenberg that it was nonsense to base a theory on observable facts alone. "In reality, the very opposite happens," he said. "It is theory which decides what we can observe."

Consider that right now you have a theory about life—a personal philosophy. Up to this point, it may have served you well. It's defined you, given you a sense of order and a way to process the world. But on the flip side, it's also been limiting you. By forming your view of yourself, others, and the world around you, it has unilaterally dictated what you see. It's told you what you can and can't do, what is and isn't possible. It's also fixed, so it continues to create whatever results you've gotten in your life up until now.

But life isn't fixed. We live in a world where we're all about updating. We update our computers, phones, cars, careers—even our partners. Now it's time to update your personal philosophy. In essence, it's time to update *you*.

This book is about transforming relationships. Not just with others, but with yourself, your experiences, your work, your purpose—how you relate to everything in your life. My aim is to give you the tools to enable you to break through the limiting views that have been keeping you stuck, frustrated, and unfulfilled. Even more, these tools will open your eyes to new possibilities and allow you to take action wherever and whenever you sense that something greater is possible. Freedom, peace, confidence, courage, love . . . it's all absolutely possible, and it all lies within the realm of being of power.

What, really, do I mean when I say "power"? That's a great question, because typically we think about it as being something we hold over someone. But I'm not talking about dominance here. I'm talking about a whole other kind of power—the kind that is generated from within for the sole purpose of leading your life from a place of strength and grace. This kind of personal power taps directly into what's important to you in your heart—what you love, what inspires you, what you cherish, what is sacred to you—and allows you to live it in whatever you do. It's the secret to being real, open, and authentic everywhere, with everyone, all the time. I know you are here because you sense that kind of power is available to you. Not a power over anyone or anything, but one *with* everyone and everything.

I know that many of you have done a lot of inner work up until picking up this book, and that's really good, because you get to keep and apply all of that. But still, the you who is reading these pages, right here, on this day, can be so greatly expanded. Something inside you knows that, doesn't it? You wouldn't be here in this moment otherwise. You've probably heard the saying, "Yesterday's enlightenment is today's ego trip." It's only in the present that you can expand, grow, and explore the bigger questions of what your life is for.

Being of Power is about enabling you to live as that expanded you—the self-actualized you, the you that you know deep down is within. Actually being of power allows you to consciously choose your response to how life, people, and events show up. You'll take responsibility for your thoughts and actions and the impact you have on your reality. You can either be like a leaf in the wind—reacting to all of your experiences from a place of "Why is this happening to me?" "Why are they doing this to me?" and even "Why does life keep showing up for me like this?"—or you can respond from a deeper reservoir of your essential self and trust that you do have a say in the matter.

The nine practices in this book are the stepping-stones on the path back to your essential authenticity, which is where your greatest power lies. I refer to them as *practices* because they are exactly that: something that one must put into action moment by moment, day by day. You won't be able to master them all at once. Instead, I'd like you to work them into each present moment, again and again, until eventually you come to exhibit them as a natural way of being. This is how to transform.

These practices didn't come together by accident, nor were they something I set out to create. Like all essential truths, they were there all along. It took many years of deep personal inquiry, searching, and a profound crisis of faith for me to discover them . . . and then many more years of practicing, teaching, and honing after that to come to live them. Do I live them perfectly, all the time? Of course not. They're a practice for me, which I continually work on. Each day, I must consciously hold the intention of embodying these principles so that I may be of my own essential power.

ॐ

For years I sensed that I was on the threshold of discovering what it is to share myself powerfully with others. My parents were pioneers in the spiritual-empowerment movement in America back in the 1960s, so I was fortunate enough to meet and study with many of the world's renowned teachers, including B.K.S. Iyengar, Bikram Choudhury, and K. Pattabhi Jois. I traveled around the world and met many other wise individuals, seeking a way of getting to the heart of life. I longed to be an exceptional teacher myself, have extraordinary relationships, and develop my potential, but I didn't know how. So I fumbled around, my brain overflowing with spiritual phrases and concepts. I did a solid yoga practice, though, and memorized verses and chapters of the Yoga Sutras. I prayed, meditated, ate raw food . . . even so, I couldn't piece together any kind of life that felt like it made any real difference to myself or others. Something important was missing.

What I know now is that having just the idea of change isn't enough. I needed to go through a series of accidental breakdowns and breakthroughs in order to shift away from a life of dogmatic discipline to one of my own personal power. It turned out that my deep need for long-term transformation put me on a collision course with myself that required a deep inquiry into my own truth. Over time, I excavated and then gradually refined a relatable, relevant methodology for whole-life metamorphosis and being of power that I now pass on to the students, teachers, and thought leaders around the world that I train—and am now presenting them to you in this book.

My aim here is not to tell you "the truth," but rather to help *you* empower what matters most to you. Your deepest power comes from what you already know inside. You have the wisdom. You have the answers. You have the heart. The nine practices of transformation will simply allow you to dissolve the blocks standing in your path and access the inner knowledge that you already possess. They will show you how to put your essential and powerful way of being into action so you can create new, expanded results everywhere and with everyone.

∽

This is not a yoga book, but it does draw on universal principles inspired from Eastern yoga practices and Western traditions of transformational training. At its core, this book is about connecting you to your best self and regenerating and re-creating who you are and what's possible. To the voices of all the wise teachers I've known and studied, I humbly add my personal experience, learning, and methodology so that anyone and everyone—yogi or not—can experience the profound joy that comes from accessing one's true power and way of being.

The practices are designed to radically reshape your perceptions, attitudes, beliefs, thought processes, feelings, and actions rather than just cause some incremental change and general self-improvement. We become of power by being bold and unflappable in our intention to transform ourselves and our world. In and of themselves, the practices don't work. *You* work! But if you work with them and let them work on you, you'll experience a whole new sense of being that's aligned to the divine.

Sadhana is a Sanskrit word that translates to "a means of accomplishing something." In a spiritual practice such as yoga, it can be a series of movements that are done in order to achieve deep transformation. Similar to yoga and the poses we use to rearrange our bodies, these are practices that we use to rearrange our inner selves and our posture in life. Each section offers a distinct practice for creating transformation of the whole.

I encourage you to read the book through once in its entirety, because the insights and information in each practice builds on the others. Having said that, it's not essential that you put them into action in any particular order. I encourage you to look at them as tools within your personal-transformation toolbox. As you make your way through them, you'll naturally find ways to apply the principles. Use whichever one speaks to you most right at that moment, and then use another when it's necessary. Each and every tool is timeless, and, therefore, always steadfast and true. You can simply draw on them one by one, as you need.

I also encourage you to be playful while being purposeful. Set the intention for growth, but hold it lightly. Often we get caught up in a goal, which can get very serious. We add heaviness and significance to it, and then this leads to all kinds of stress. Remember that our objective here is to expand with love and joy, which comes from doing the work with lightness in our hearts. I often see newer yoga students struggling as they attempt Tree Pose (a balancing pose) because they don't have balance yet. They fall and get frustrated, and a lot of energy goes into the drama of "failing." But as we mature in the practice, we can just say, "Oh, I was in Tree Pose, and I fell out. No big deal." We can laugh and then just resume where we left off. That's what I mean about still being on purpose but being light. Can you feel how much more room for growth and freedom there is in that?

Since truths are timeless, you may have heard some of what you'll encounter in this book before. But as we'll talk about in "Practice #1: Be a Yes," can you be open to hearing and experiencing them in a new way? Can you open your mind and your heart to a greater expansion beyond what you already know? My guess is that the answer is indeed yes, just by virtue of the fact that you're reading this book.

There is so much more for us to discover beyond our current knowledge, if we're willing to reframe perceptions and try on ideas in a new way. So for now, suspend what you already know. It's all still in there, and as I said, you get to keep all that insight and wisdom. The question now that those of us who are up to something bigger need to ask is always, "What's next?"

In the spirit of discovery, learning, and teaching, I'm sharing this work with you so you can find your true north. I am a teacher who wishes to awaken *your* inner teacher and your own discovery of what works for you. So let's begin. You are ready now to come face-to-face with what's going on in your heart and in your life. Let's take the journey together of exploring the nine practices of transformation. What lies ahead is the possibility of fresh pathways and a whole new kind of power to light up yourself, your life, and your entire world.

———⌇———

BE A YES

*"Yes is a world
& in this world of
yes live
(skillfully curled)
all worlds"*

— E. E. CUMMINGS

A big part of the work I do involves leading weeklong trainings for people who want to learn to teach Baptiste Yoga, be leaders in their communities, and experience personal transformation. On the surface, these are yoga-teacher trainings, but really they're about individuals breaking through to their real power by clearing out whatever is blocking them from being the most natural, authentic expression of themselves and creating an extraordinary life. People come from all over the world—Europe, Asia, South America, Canada, and even Africa—to participate in seven full days of transformational training, boot-camp style.

But just because the participants have paid their money, have gotten on a plane, and are sitting in their seat or on their mat doesn't mean that they're fully committed. Just getting themselves into that training room isn't always enough to guarantee that they're fully *there*. I've done hundreds of trainings, and nearly every time those first three days are like trying to swim through molasses. Right along with their excitement and passion, participants bring their resistance, fears, cynicism, and resignation.

Although people begin having mini breakthroughs right away, it's usually not until day three when each person experiences a bigger, deeper shift in energy. That's when we get to one of the most important practices of the week: committing to the program. The students engage in an exercise where they use the power of their word as a commitment to create their reality as possibility. It's at this pivotal point that the lights start going on and real transformation begins.

I call this internal commitment "being a yes." This practice sets the platform for all the others in the book. Without the inner yes that's needed to create the context and commitment to transform, it's as if you never get past the word *go*. All the other practices will fall flat if you aren't open to the power that's available to you by being a yes and taking action with the tools. This is not about positive thinking or sugarcoating anything in feel-good goo. It's about being confident in your ability to turn difficulty into possibility, upsets into positive energy, and breakdowns into breakthroughs.

Yes is an energetic place. When you're coming from this energy, it alters and impacts the way you see yourself, your life, your thoughts, and your feelings. It shapes your actions right here in the present moment.

For example, think about how your view changes and your actions are shaped when there's a new relationship in your life that excites you. Or when you start planning a dream vacation or learn that you're getting an exciting, new opportunity at work that will lift you up to a new level. You begin to perceive your circumstances in a new light. Your patterns of thought and emotion align themselves with fulfilling the new pathway that you're able to now see right in front of you. When being a yes, you're someone who is standing positively for what's happening in your life and for what you want to have happen in your future—you're a person who's up to something bigger. *Yes* sets the stage for being of power.

The Dance of Yes and No

We are either a yes or a no. For a lot of us, somewhere along the way, we started out a yes and became a no. A natural skepticism is, of course, healthy and necessary. When I was younger, I was very wary of gurus and New Age teachers, and I think that reluctance made me more purposefully think things through and choose the path, teachers, and life direction that best served what I needed at each point. My suspicion allowed me to take a stand for what I felt was right for me.

Sometimes our ability to say no actually serves our bigger yes. There is no claim to virtue without the clear-cut ability to say no to things that don't support what we're up to. If you're a yes for possibility, that means you're also saying no to resignation, cynicism, and self-sabotage. If you're a yes for honest and true communication, you're a no for things such as gossip. Closing off one opens the other; this is the dance of yes and no. Those points of no are important for grounding. If you're all yes all the time for everyone in your life—which I hear a lot of people say they are—what authentically matters most to you is harder to distinguish and likely isn't getting served. Thus, no can be a valuable tool for setting boundaries.

Having said that, and without realizing it, a lot of us tend to be *overly* wary—even cynical—to a point that limits what's possible and holds us back from growth. It's part of our routine to automatically and rigidly say no to life: "No, I can't do that." "No, that won't work . . . I've tried it before." "No, that's not possible. This is just the way things are/the way I am."

I see this all the time in yoga students. They'll say, "Oh, I can't do that," "No, I'm not flexible enough," "I don't do headstands," or whatever their "no" pose is. They get so conditioned to "I don't do that," that years and years can go by and they never even attempt it. But then maybe some teacher challenges them in a different way or they're suddenly inspired to try it, and it's like *Whoosh, up you go!* They didn't even know they'd moved past whatever physical or mental block was in their way. They went from a rigid, limiting belief about themselves into a revelation that something more was possible.

Remember how I said earlier that our thoughts, feelings, and actions are shaped by our context? It's also important to know that we can only act within the boundaries of that existing environment. Our so-called weaknesses or inabilities can often be products of some disempowering limitation that blinds us to our real power. We limit what's possible when we look at the world from inside the comfortable box that we call our familiar reality or "the world as I know it." Wherever we're restricted in life, we've created a situation that's holding that limitation in place, even if we can't see it. We have a blind spot.

The problem is that most of us come from being a no when it comes to this kind of self-inquiry, so we automatically reject the idea that we have blind spots and never see these hidden limitations. We feel that we're trying our best in life, and while things might not be great, they are as good as they can be for now. This subtle resignation further keeps our obstructions held in place.

My question for you is this: can you be open, especially in the areas where you're currently closed, and be a yes to uncovering your blind spots? Can you hold in your heart that idea of being a yes even if it feels uncomfortable and make it a moment-to-moment routine as you try the different tools in this book? You may be tempted to skip over some of the practices if they sound like something you've heard before. But if everything you've been doing so far has only gotten you to where you are, can you see the wisdom in attempting something that perhaps you've already tried but doing it in a new way? Are you open to listening from a new place within yourself?

The Inner Battle

There is an old Cherokee legend that says we each have two wolves battling for dominance inside of us: a good wolf and a bad wolf. Both desperately want to win. The bad wolf represents the inner voice that speaks to us from a place of survival and scarcity—from doubt, failure, regret, envy, self-pity, false pride, and resentment. It conjures up thoughts like *It's my fault, I'm to blame, I'm not good enough,* and *I'm all alone.* The bad wolf stands for our inner no of resignation and cynicism.

The good wolf stands for our yes of possibility and represents the inner voice of truth—the quiet, still place of inner knowing. Joy, love, integrity, power, peace, abundance, freedom, compassion, and generosity emerge from that good wolf. Its voice whispers from the heart, "Who I am is whole and complete."

The lesson of this legend is that whichever wolf we feed gets stronger and wins. We could also call this a crisis between the real you and the not you. *The real you exists in a state of calm empowerment; the not you doubts, blames, worries, resents, and distrusts itself and the world around it.* We can make this crisis conscious and let it transform us by shining light on our blind spots and the areas of our lives where we're hiding, stuck, shut down, and inauthentic.

When we're standing in our power, we purposefully create an inner revolution. Rather than living from an outdated context and waiting for life to bring us crashing to our knees, we bring the floor up and cause an intentional spiritual crisis by disrupting business as usual. We give up the resignation, stir the bottom of the barrel, declare a new way, and take a stand for an extraordinary life in which we experience authentic power. This is how we feed the good wolf in us and starve the bad one.

There is a process I use in my trainings to help students distinguish between the voices of the good wolf and the bad wolf. I recommend trying this, even for just one day, to see what opens up for you:

> Choose an area of your life where the energy is either somewhat stuck or totally shut down. The first one that comes to mind is usually the one to focus on, since it's foremost in your consciousness. Now take out a piece of paper and write down the worries, concerns, complaints, or negative thoughts that are running in the background of your mind about that part of your life

right now. These are the voice of the bad wolf, the survival mind. They say, *It's my fault. It's their fault. It shouldn't be this way. No, never, not possible. I can't change this—it's just how things are. I can't deal with this. It's not worth the risk of failing, being left alone, or causing trouble. This exercise is stupid. I don't want to waste my time doing it.*

Don't judge your thoughts or filter them in any way; just tell the truth, and get it down on paper. You're listening, not to empower them, but instead to notice their presence so you can begin to separate them out and dissolve them.

Next, look for any positive inner sense or thoughts. Get really calm, notice your feet on the floor, and observe if there's even a tiny sense of "something new is possible" percolating up from deep within your being. Write those thoughts down, too. This is the voice of the good wolf, your inspired intuition, the real you. It says, *Yes. Go for it. Take the risk. I can do this even if I don't know how right it is at this moment. Game on.* There is the presence of an inner yes, a sense of being okay even if all outward signs indicate otherwise. This voice has energy and aliveness. It feels expansive and peaceful, even in the presence of fear.

As you observe your inner reality, you may notice that the bad wolf is there—a lot or just a little—nudging you to stay in the shadows. But the good wolf is also there, encouraging you to come out into the light. The bad wolf whispers, *Don't trust. Don't reveal yourself. You'll look stupid.*

You're not good enough. Hide, lie, pretend. . . . Yet at the same time, the good wolf is communicating to you in the wordless language of the heart: *Why be afraid? You are loved. Be courageous. Be real. Be of power. You are worthy. Take a stand. Have faith. Trust.*

By paying attention for a day, you'll see that the head has its own voice, as does the heart, which asks questions like, "What really matters to me in life?" "Who do I aspire to be?" "What do I value?" and "Who am I choosing to be for others and for myself?"

The head is not at all engaged in that kind of inquiry. It's always listening to the sea of its own opinions and saying, "What's in it for me?" It hears through the filters of what's familiar and has kept you safe in the past. It tells you all the reasons why you cannot do what you dream of doing. It says, "I'm tired, and I don't even care whether or not I have an empowered life. Maybe I will someday."

To this day, when I am having a conversation with someone or leading a training, I work at staying conscious to the questions such as, "Who [or what] in me is talking right now? Who is listening right now?" With practice, we get clearer about which wolf is present as we speak and listen, and we can consciously choose which one we want to feed and strengthen.

Taking Your Seat

Regardless of your circumstances, if you're a yes for possibility and declare it, embody it, and align yourself to the vision that inspires you, this creates energy within you and around you that will bring your intention into reality. In yoga we call this "taking your seat." Gandhi called it "being the change."

Your success in anything is ultimately a matter of intention. Committing to an intention is powerful because it pushes you to grow into something. You have a clear vision of "I'm going to do that" or "I'm going to be that." Once you dedicate yourself in this way, you put both feet in, both buns down, and, somehow, you have to dig deeper. You draw out an inner kind of strength and confidence to create your life more powerfully. Isn't that what you're here for?

One of the barriers that many of us run up against in ourselves is an avoidance of making commitments that could shift our compass in new directions. Let's face it: we may be uncomfortable or even unhappy living inside the box we've created for ourselves, but at least we know our way around in there. There's a tendency to stay vague about what we want and act somewhat tranquilized, because we know in our guts that the motivation and power to break out of the box comes from clarity.

One of my students told a story about how she avoided questioning what she wanted in a romantic relationship, since deep down she knew that if she took that kind of inquiry to the situation she'd have to end it. How many of us have been there or in a similar situation, be it in our relationships, our jobs, or any other life circumstances? The head avoids clarity at all costs, because being clear takes us into the unknown and can get risky. This is a very important point, one worth reinforcing: *Our power to create at the next level of any area in our lives lies in our clarity.*

I have students who say, "I want to have a breakthrough." Well, that's great, but it's not enough. A breakthrough in what? You want to get really specific here. Think of an area in your life where you would like to see progress. Maybe it's in your work, relationships, or overall way of being. For some people, it can be about having closure regarding something from the past or getting peace of mind around a troubling issue. It could even be making progress toward happiness, inspiration, or courage. Just get very clear on what it is, and spell it out. Write: *I commit to having a breakthrough in* _____. If you want to get powerful in your life, you have to ask for it. Putting it down on paper is like penning a wish list to the universe.

When you commit in this way, you create an opening, and into that opening little fragments of light start to filter through. It's not magic; it's a matter of awareness. For example, when you're thinking about buying a certain kind of car, all of a sudden you start to notice that same make and model showing up everywhere you go. Breakthroughs happen exactly like that. You simply open yourself up for one, which clears a pathway for grace to come in. We'll talk about that a little more in "Practice #4: Give It Up to Get Empty"—about how we create space for grace. For now, all I want you to do is commit to your intention: to be a yes with your full heart and let the rest of the tools in this book do their work on you as you engage with them.

Want vs. Ready

It was day five of a teacher training in Mexico. A student stood up at the mic to share something, and since speaking and sharing in front of the group was an everyday part of the training, I was a little surprised that I didn't recognize her. I quickly found out why.

"This is my seventh Baptiste teacher training," she said, with a tone of quiet confidence. Her whole being was radiating grounded presence. "I've come to six others, and throughout all six, I've never stood to speak—not once. Each training has given me amazing results, but I kept coming back specifically because I wanted to have a breakthrough in my fear of speaking in front of the group. Up until now, I'd convinced myself that I wasn't ready. But now I *am* ready!"

There is no "you" that can't do something that seems possible. There are only thoughts and feelings that pop up and try to stop you. The truth is that you're always ready, right now. The thing that inspires you deep in your heart is what you're ready for. Anything else you believe is just a story that you made up about how you can't—one that's dictated by the bad wolf and kept alive by a fear-fueled inner no. If you're reading this book, it means that you're up to something bigger in your life, and whatever breakthrough is on the horizon, you're ready for it—right here, right now. This is it. The beginning of being of power is when we move away from "Someday, maybe, I want to . . ." to "I am committed to _____." Anything that's really important to you, any result that you really want for yourself that you can envision as a possibility, is not a maybe/someday/however kind of thing.

How we language our intention has a big impact. What we want to get to here is the distinction between "I want" and "I am." Many of us can spend years in "I want," as in, "I want to lose 20 pounds," or "I want to fly an airplane." "I'm trying to lose 20 pounds" is very different from "I am losing 20 pounds in 10 weeks, 2 pounds a week" and actually doing the practices that create the real results. Sure, I may want to fly an airplane . . . someday. But if I'm really ready to do so, I'll do the research, find an instructor, and take lessons—whatever it takes. Simply wishing or hoping to do something doesn't work. When we make a statement as a wish or a desire for someday, but not now, it yields little results. We must either commit to doing something or not. It's that simple.

A practice I use with my students to shift away from the vagueness of "want" into the clarity of "ready now" is claiming the power of declaration. When we speak with directness—"This is who I am and what I'm committed to"—and your heart is in it, you're using the power of your word to integrate who you are, your way of seeing, your thoughts, your feelings, and your actions. You're lining up the forces inside and around you. When you declare what's important with focus, intention, and clarity, you create new pathways of possibility. The action of declaration works.

We'll use this practice a few times throughout this book, but for now, it's enough to just begin to play with the energetic power of declaration. A student at a training recently told me, "I just want to let go of having to be strong all the time." I asked if she was open to being coached on that, and she said yes, so I asked her to drop the "I just want to" and instead use "I give up having to be strong all the time." As soon as she said this, she seemed to embody a sense of ease and confidence.

Claiming something, even if right now you don't fully believe it to be true, sparks a brighter quality of aliveness in the body. Go ahead and try it. Think of an area of your life in which you desire a breakthrough. Say it out loud first with "I want" in front of it. Maybe it's "I want to find a new job that I love" or "I want to get healthy." Now drop the "I want" and replace it with "I am" (or "I will"). This time, say, "I am attracting work that I love and the financial resources to support me fully," or even, simply, "I will find a new job that I love." Can you feel the difference? That subtle distinction in language will make a tremendous difference in your capacity to transform.

The beauty of this is that you really don't even need to believe it—not right now. That's not what this is about. Actually, whether you believe it or not is irrelevant. It's like gravity; you don't have to believe in it, but does that mean it doesn't exist? Being intentional and declaring what you're up to *as though it is already in existence and happening in reality* creates an energetic shift. Little by little, you start showing up in a new way—everywhere and with everyone. You just stand for your intended result and act from that. This is how you transform. Not by hoping, willing, or trying, but by establishing the space within yourself for a breakthrough into a new place of possibility. You construct your reality from that new way of being without any resistance to it, and soon it's no longer a question of believing, because what you want shows up right in front of you as a tangible result.

What Takes You Out?

The idea in yoga practice is that you just do it. Do it from awareness, but just do it. You get on your mat and through doing, breathing, and working the tools, you start having these deep fundamental shifts. Things start opening, strengthening, and shifting in body and being, because you're engaging. But—and this is a big but—we can only have those kinds of breakthroughs if we stay in the practice.

Whether you're on the yoga mat or in everyday life, right in the moment when you're about to have a breakthrough, one of two things happen: The heat—what we call *Shiva's fire*—roars in and blows the lid off, and you have some kind of opening in your awareness or your body. You experience that essential moment where you break through into a new place, a new world, a new freedom and vitality, a whole new awareness in which you see yourself and your life in a different light. Or, cold air kicks in right before you're pierced by that magic moment, and you take yourself out.

It's amazing how many students suddenly have to use the restroom as soon as the pose they hate the most comes up. It's as if they say, "Oh, now's a good time for me to go." I'm not saying you shouldn't get up to go to the bathroom if you need to. If you've got to go, then go—there's no story to it, you've just got to go, right? But if there's something else, like finding an exit in a moment of difficulty, then that's the time to stay right where you are, because it's a signal that you're right on the verge of breaking through.

When the resistance comes up and we stay rather than run, feel rather than flee, we find those golden portals of growth. Our resistance dissolves by relaxing with what is and holding that space for something new to open up. In the Baptiste community, we have a saying: "If you can, you must." This a great tool that gives us access to our deep wells of courage and dissolves our resistance in the moments when we feel tempted to give up.

The word *courage* comes from the Latin root *cor,* meaning "heart." To be courageous means to live with and from the heart. Being of power means we drop the safety and cushion of reasons and excuses. It's important to understand that bravery isn't the same as fearlessness. The practice of courage is feeling fear and acting anyway in the face of it. It's being a yes when the bad wolf is howling for you to run away, hide, control, resist, or say no. It's the pathway to authenticity and personal power.

Ultimately, what will sabotage and stop you from authoring a new way in any area of your life is the little voice in your head that says, "This good result won't last," "Why bother?" or "Who are you kidding? This is stupid." You want to stay aware and notice when this pops up to stop you. Your job is to get powerful at *giving it up and letting it go* every time you see, hear, and feel the voice of the bad wolf rear its ugly head.

Will you have setbacks and moments when the road gets especially tough? Of course. As the famous yoga master and my teacher B.K.S. Iyengar says, "No thorns, no roses." Being of power requires the courage to keep moving through those thorny patches that can cause us to spiral down and away from the radiant realm of what's possible. It happens to everyone. Those times are exactly when we need to take our seat, realign, and recommit, again and again.

The answer to how is always yes. Can you be a yes, not just here in the beginning, but always and forever?

RELEASE THE CONCERN FOR LOOKING GOOD

"Don't be fooled by me
Don't be fooled by the face I wear
For I wear a mask, a thousand masks,
Masks that I'm afraid to take off,
And none of them is me.

"Pretending is an art that's second nature with me,
But don't be fooled,
For God's sake don't be fooled.
I give you the impression that I'm secure,
That all is sunny and unruffled with me, within as well
As without,
That confidence is my name and coolness my game,
That the water's calm and I'm in command
And that I need no one,
But don't believe me. . . ."

— CHARLES C. FINN

The lines above are from a poem called "Please Hear What I'm Not Saying." It's one of my favorites, because it cuts to the heart of the one thing so many of us do that blocks our power, which is to hide.

We hide behind our competency: our degrees, our knowledge, our advanced yoga poses, our successes, the things we're good at . . . what makes us feel safe. We cover up our insecurities and fears because we're afraid of showing anything other than the "everything is A-OK in here" façade to the world. That concern for looking good (and, conversely, not looking bad) drives so much of what we do. But it's also what stands in the way of us being real.

Concealing at any level always comes at a cost: peace of mind, a sense of freedom, our health, or vitality in our physical body, to name a few. When we're without authenticity, we're not being ourselves—our energy is stuck. It gets contracted because so much is going toward covering up what we don't want people to see; what we don't want to deal with; or whatever judgments we have about not being good enough, smart enough, strong enough, or *anything* enough.

Imagine right now if you were to be open, undefended, and fully transparent in every part of your life. Can you picture how freeing it would be to give up all the pretending and just be out there, exactly as you are, without any masks? That might seem scary, but you're here to transform, so game on!

The greatest source of natural power we have available to us is being ourselves. Our lives are transformed when we bring that organic way of self-expression to all of our relationships and experiences. Most of us already know that the word *yoga* means "union," and to me the biggest union is the alignment between who we are at our core and how we show up in the world. When we drop the masks and live from our authenticity, we ignite our power and our whole life opens up.

Facing the Fear of Failure

I once saw a news story on Michael Jordan in which he talked about how he would review his performance after each basketball game. He would watch tapes of himself and only look for one thing, which was where he was failing or his technique was ineffective. He didn't hold on to his mistakes as a sign that something was wrong with him. Instead, he saw them as an opportunity to up his game and grow in excellence. Seeing mistakes empowered him; owning failure was his pathway to greatness.

And even though we might not all be professional athletes, we live in the same "get the job done or fail" world as Jordan. Rather than deal with the possible embarrassment that comes with putting ourselves out there, we shrink away from being at risk and making mistakes. We instead give lots of justifications for why we should stay in our comfort zone.

For the most part, we have almost no training in how to deal with failure. Therefore, moving into the unknown is a threat to us. If we look up *failure* in the dictionary, it says, "The state or condition of not meeting a desirable or intended objective." How threatening does that sound? Not very, right? Well, that's all it really is. But for us human beings, it's way more emotionally charged than simply the lack of achieving a result. For us, failure isn't about an unachieved task, a relationship that didn't work out, or a poorly taught or practiced yoga class. It's about what it means to us if we're considered a failure and how others see us. There is only one thing worse than "I failed," and that is, "I am a failure." *I am* turns it into a declaration about our very existence as human beings, not a statement about how we showed up on the mat, on the court, or in the trenches of life.

All of that self-condemnation comes up, and we become afraid of taking risks or focusing on doing things right or not at all. But we have the ability to break free from that. *We can embrace the possibility of failure. We can see it as a rich part of our learning process and trust that every breakdown leads to a breakthrough, to new pathways of action. Releasing that fear of inadequacy opens up a whole other level of freedom. And in freedom lies power.*

I'm not saying this lightly, believe me. In my life today, I teach and speak in front of thousands of people. When I was younger and first started, though, presenting to groups was really hard for me. One of the biggest fears I used to have was of being perceived negatively. As soon as I walked into the room to begin a workshop or class, my hands would perspire, my heart would race, and I'd hear all kinds of self-critical commentary running through my head: *You shouldn't have said that. They don't like you. You're messing up.*

When I started giving public lectures and teaching to large groups, I'd barely pull them off because my anxiety was so fierce. I'd lose my train of thought, rush my comments, or launch into performance mode because I was more worried about what people would think rather than being intentional and straightforward from the heart. I gave a good appearance of being competent and even authentic, but I really wasn't because I was so consumed by my concern for doing it right. Generally, I was fearful during the entire experience, and this didn't match the picture of how I wanted to be. I'd do my best, but that was very different than being myself.

What I didn't understand at the time was how primal this concern for looking good was and how it was blocking my natural expression and ability to speak from the heart. Standing up and presenting to a group was threatening to my very survival—not because my body was in real danger, but because it carried the risk of embarrassment.

It took me many, many years to feel comfortable in my own skin, and it was ultimately the practice of learning to dissolve the fear when it came up that helped me get past this issue. I would practice identifying and locating the fear in my body, and then feeling and experiencing it fully until it loosened its grip on me. I was able to practice this whenever it came up and finally discovered the freedom to fully express myself from an authentic place. Little by little, I broke through my apprehension and found my rhythm. Eventually, I started loving the experience of connecting with people and sharing ideas and transformational practices with large groups. Today, I feel a genuine sense of ease and flow when I'm in front of a crowd, be they made up of 10 people or 10,000. It's just me up there, expressing fully and sharing what inspires me without any sense of constraint.

The Anatomy of Failure

Why on earth would you resist being of power? What's to be feared that would make living in a comfort zone more appealing? Like me, you're probably up to some extraordinary things and being bold in certain areas, possibly even empowering others to do the same. That's not in question. The bottom-line question on the table is this: Why do you resist being fully in your power in *all* areas of your life?

The answer is actually very simple. You, me, and human beings in general resist the clarity and power that come from being, living, acting, speaking, and creating from our authentic truth so that we don't have to deal with failure. Rather than risk looking bad, we will sacrifice what's in our heart.

As a young yoga teacher, I cultivated my own way of sharing my practice in a form that inspired me. For the most part, no one in the traditional yoga world understood me: They tended to shake their heads at me and what I taught, telling me that it wasn't yoga, spiritual, or deep enough to last—that Baptiste Power Yoga would be a passing trend. I took a lot of hits and had a lot of failures along the way, but I didn't stop. I knew I wanted to create a system and a new kind of revolutionary work in the world of self-development and transformation. I wanted it to have commercial value so that it could reach a lot of people, especially those who typically would not have access. So I kept following my heart and what felt true to me.

My parents, Walt and Magaña Baptiste, were my primary mentors and models for how to stand in the face of scrutiny and criticism. As a kid, I watched them both go through the fire as pioneers in the world of holistic health, modern yoga, and spiritual transformation. Growing up around Dad's work as a revolutionary personal-development guru seemed perfectly normal to me. But to the real world it was unusual and definitely before its time, and to most it bordered on the bizarre. It seemed to me like my parents were offering something of such great value to people, so it was difficult to understand all the resistance.

For me they modeled being a yes for what matters most in one's heart and giving up the concern for what people think. They taught me to let people throw stones but keep my eyes on the prize of what's possible. You will fail, but when you're committed, you don't quit. You find a way to make those failures strengthen you. You take the lessons and up your game.

Being who you truly are in your power without the masks means stepping outside the sea of the same old thing and risking having others judge you or even see you as less than perfect. It's unavoidable that growth is messy; if you put yourself out there, you'll absolutely have difficult moments. There's no risk in hiding and playing it safe, and there's also no power.

So what if you fail? Can you take risks and use failures and mistakes as opportunities for learning and upping your game? Can you create new pathways and possibilities for yourself, knowing that some will work out the way you imagined (or even beyond that) and some won't, and make it your practice to allow for both outcomes to be enlightening stepping-stones to what's next? Can you give up the concern for looking good, knowing that it's what stands between you and your ability to evolve?

Being Yourself Opens Up New Space to Create

In order to create new pathways in any area of your life, you must get real wherever you haven't been. Acknowledging what's stuck and telling the truth about where you've been wearing a mask opens up new energy to flow in the present.

The problem is that most of us refuse to admit that we are not being ourselves in the areas of our life that matter most. Automatic denial keeps us from seeing any inauthenticity that's the source of resistance and causes stuckness, and this is where we need to dig deeper and find the courage to risk getting real with ourselves.

Regardless of how you feel about it, any area of your life where the energy is stuck or contracted or you feel disempowered has some inauthenticity present. Perhaps you can't see it, but it's there! If you can locate and tell the truth about it, you access great energetic freedom. It opens up the future like blank pages in a book, available to be filled by new ways of being.

Being inauthentic is not bad or wrong—it's just not real. Without blame or embarrassment, your practice here is to confront, layer by layer, one after the other, each area of your life that lacks genuineness and start coming clean about it. The breakthrough occurs by getting into action and restoring transparency and truth. If you're anything like me, you probably don't like looking at the areas where you have been insincere and how this has impacted your life in unwanted ways. But I know that not looking at them won't make them go away. I've learned that looking at the ugly stuff and taking responsibility for it is an essential practice for living an extraordinary life.

Where Are You Hiding?

Consider just for a moment that every bone in your body is inauthentic. I'm not saying that it is, but just *consider* it for a moment. Start from the idea that you're not being yourself in every area of your life. Go through your whole being, bone by bone, each one representing an area or a relationship, and ask yourself, "Am I hiding here? Am I pretending things are one way, but really they're another? Am I being real, or am I acting?"

The point of this exercise isn't to make all sorts of judgments or condemn yourself, but to set yourself free. So just put the chastisement aside, and get really clear about where you're hiding and pretending and where you're being real. Go through your entire existence: your relationships, your work, your family, your health, your financial life, how you show up in groups of people and the world at large—all of it. A big clue that you're caught up in the concern for looking good is if you're burned out, stuck, deadened, resistant, or experiencing a loss of purpose or inner peace. That's a signal that somewhere in there the real you is missing. When you feel that way, your energy flow is blocked in some way, and that leaves you drained.

I'm not saying that it's easy to call ourselves out like this. Believe me, I get it; we've put a lot of energy into covering up our insecurities or whatever other flaws we don't want people to see. One of my students recently said, "I feel embarrassed being straight with people. I don't want to admit that I don't have it all together the way they think I do." It's like that for many of us, and that's why we keep wearing masks. We want others to admire us. So why would we own up to things that would get us anything other than admiration?

In turn, we just start pretending, and before long we forget we're doing so. It's similar to wearing glasses: You're aware that you're using them when you first put them on, but when you do all the time, you forget about them. You see through the lenses, and although they're altering your vision, you somehow don't remember that they're there. You forget that you're pretending, and in your mind this perspective becomes who you are.

These filters control and limit us, because we don't even know what we don't know. When we bring one into view and say, "Hey, yeah, I'm not telling the truth" or I'm pretending here," suddenly now it doesn't have us in its grip—*we* have *it*. We hold it differently because we're aware; we're awake to ourselves not being real.

It's way more powerful to be conscious of yourself as a fraud, if you are, rather than hiding the fact that you're not. Pretending is toxic, and it's the energy of disease. Do you want to create inner peace, freedom, and an empowered life that's full of true joy and happiness? Then make it a practice to be real, shoot straight, and tell yourself the truth from a context of empowerment.

When I got to a point where I started to really see how I'd been treating my family and the people around me, it was as if a light switched on. I got it. Similar to that moment when the meaning of a joke dawns on you and you laugh, I had this "aha!" moment and suddenly saw where I'd been out of alignment. I realized that up to that point I'd been living in a world of blame, fault, and resentment, and now I was able to clearly see the cost and impact that all of this had on my life.

A deep sadness ran through me . . . really deep. And also a kind of gladness, too, because I thought, *Whoa, it's a relief to see this now.* I saw it as good news. The truth really did give me a new sense of freedom. Waking up to it allowed me to finally begin shifting out of my false self. In my heart I knew I had a lot of talent and gifts to share with the world, but the constraint of all the self-imposed drama and conflict I carried from my past had greatly limited my power and self-expression. I simply hadn't stepped it up to the degree that I'd wanted to. Out of the discovery that I wasn't being real, I was free to be myself and fully commit to new practices and clear new pathways. I started to show up for myself as more power-ful, connected, and aware of the potential for flow in my life. Much the same as when I was a young child, I started to believe again that anything is possible.

It's empowering to be in a place where you can be real with everyone in your life. Otherwise, you're betraying yourself, which is a big hit to your vitality.

The lighter side of this practice of examining every energetic bone in your body is that you'll simultaneously realize all your genuine qualities. You get to look at some and say, "Oh, this one's authentic, actually. This one . . . okay, I like that, it works. I like how I'm being in my [work, relationships, connections with people, and so on]. But this one over here . . . no, that's not powerful and doesn't serve me. That's a place where I'm hiding and want to uncover my freedom and power." Go through and see yourself clearly, and then, from that vantage point of clarity, you can see what's fulfilling you and also the work you need to do.

Where are you hiding? Where do you pretend? What are you covering up? And, most important, at what cost?

Creating Fearless Connections

"I was always worried about people finding out that I wasn't good enough," shared Susan, a 45-year-old mother and workshop participant. "I was worried about having to cover everything up, and by doing that, I was keeping myself from having true connections with others. Here I was surrounded by people I loved, and who I knew loved me, but I felt so lonely all the time because I wasn't really being myself when I was with them."

Sound familiar?

I've heard countless students talk about an endless array of "flaws" that they're afraid of exposing. They're afraid of just being themselves, because they think others will judge or reject them. You may not think that your friends see or feel it when you're hiding something, but at some level they do. People can sense everything, and whether consciously or not, on some level they know when they're not getting the real *you*.

If someone gets too close, we panic that they'll see what's underneath the mask, so we go right into survival mode. We defend ourselves, create distance, resist, avoid, even wave the phony "peace, love, and compassion flag." We keep others out by making sure we look good in their eyes. If our strategies fail, we default into making them wrong. We think we're protecting ourselves by putting up walls, but in reality we're the ones creating our own prisons.

In some of my leadership and teacher-training programs, we do an exercise where we have participants stand up in the front of the classroom to face the group and teach. Suddenly, I'll call out, "Pause." Then the trainee will simply stand there not saying or doing anything, but just looking at the individuals right in front of him or her in the classroom. Almost immediately, those who are "on display" start fidgeting, giggling, and averting their eyes—anything to not have to look at the people in front of them, and in turn because they're being seen so simply, intimately, and without pretense.

But they stay. (Well, they stay because they have to . . . it's part of the training. I'm guessing about 95 percent of them would run if I gave them the option.) Then they hold a gaze with the other participants without talking. The intention is to really see each other.

What starts to happen as students do this exercise is that the masks drop and the protective walls they've built up over the years start to dissolve. They stand as a mirror for each other as all the pent-up, stuffed-down energy comes up and out, until they find themselves standing there with their pure humanity exposed. If it sounds scary, that's because it is. There are plenty of tears, laughter, and sometimes even raw, wracking sobs; being seen in this kind of way causes all kinds of breakdowns and breakthroughs. But always there is a shining release of energy and a palpable sense of lightness at the end.

Jessica, a 21-year-old participant, described her experience this way: "I've always compared myself to other people. I judge myself and make myself inferior . . . I'm not smart enough, not thin enough, and not educated enough. All these things constantly go through my head. Connecting with others in this exercise was really hard for me at first, but when I started seeing them beyond just their surface appearance, I realized that we can get and give incredible power from each other when we stop hiding. It didn't matter anymore what I looked like, what I drove, or where I went to school. I can be myself, and I don't need to hide. All that judgment feels as if it's gone now . . . like I can exhale and suddenly see my whole world through new eyes."

Now *that* is a breakthrough! A breakthrough is when you step through some energetic veil to where what was limiting you is now behind you and you're standing in a completely new space. Creating fearless connection with others in your life transports you out from behind your self-created walls. You discover the ability to relate to people more deeply and from your purest, fullest, most unfettered way of being.

Now, I get that you're not going to walk around looking deeply into everyone's eyes. I mean, that would be weird. The way we break down the barriers is through an even simpler practice: *being transparent and telling the truth from the heart*. Always. Everywhere. With everyone. Try that on for a minute. Imagine how freeing it would be to not have to keep pretending that everything is okay, that you've got it all together and figured out. To some, that might seem like a weakness, but this kind of transparency is actually a huge source of strength, because all your aliveness is no longer bound up in creating smoke screens. Great reservoirs of energy become available to you as you stand front and center in your power and are straight in your communication.

This is the practice I offer you to take on. Begin to tell the truth to yourself about where the energy is stuck and where you are hiding, pretending, and lying in your life, intimate relationships, work environment, and family or home life. It's important that you do this without embarrassment and without invalidating yourself or anyone else.

From this position of bravery and clarity, move into action to get the energy unstuck in those areas by restoring your genuine self with people. Have heart-to-heart, face-to-face conversations, and acknowledge where you've been withholding how things really are for you. When and where it's needed, apologize, ask for forgiveness, appreciate the good things someone has done for you, and hold out a new promise for your relationships and what you are now committed to bringing in that's new (as in, "I am now committed to being _____ with/for/to you"). Open up the communication with the individuals you need to clean things up with, and create new pathways of relating that empower.

What you want to get here is that this is a *practice*—a new way of being that you will embody with more and more mastery over time. If you have something to say, say it. If you feel tempted to lie or cover something up in the name of looking good or hiding, quickly remind yourself that inauthenticity never works. Never. It's also helpful to ask yourself in those moments, "Do I really want to make a mess of my life again in this way?" and "What am I so afraid of, and what is it costing me?" Chances are that it's costing you your power, peace of mind, and what you really want for yourself. By the way, something to consider is that other people are far less concerned with you than you might think. They're all too focused on worrying about how they look in *your* eyes to worry about you.

It can seem scary at first to do this with individuals whom you haven't had open, transparent communication with up until now. But I'll tell you something that I've learned: You can actually create how other people in your life will show up around you. When you speak from the heart, you speak into the hearts of others. You relate to everyone else as if they have an open heart, even if theirs has been closed or bound up. The truth always stands up to anything, and we have to trust that. Transformed people are those who can be completely themselves, and they in turn create a transformed environment where truth and transparency can be shared and expressed freely.

One of the practices in the world of Baptiste Yoga is that we relate to people *as if they are already in their power,* whether they're already there or not. We don't focus on their stuckness or lack, but instead support them in realizing what they really care about and the results they want to achieve, in the process leaving them empowered with new practices. My point here is that if you approach everyone from a generous place—from your own open, truthful heart and with the intention of giving them power—then you create space for everyone around you to also show up in that way. They'll hear you and, in their own way, start coming out of hiding and relate to you in a new way; before you know it, you'll start thinking what a coincidence it is that you're surrounded by all these like-minded people. But they may not have started out that way. Consider that your courageous heart opened theirs—that they mirrored you. Yes, you really are that powerful.

Once you begin shifting and come from truth when breakdowns, frustrations, or judgments arise, you immediately recognize that you don't want to be participating in that negativity. You can stop the dynamic right there in its tracks and say, "I'm sorry. Let's pause here. Let's re-create this." You lead the change.

But none of this—not one single piece—is possible if you're hiding and not relating to others from your full truth. Where can you strip away the walls and stand face-to-face with those in your life, sharing what you're committed to openly? Where can you inspire them and yourself to be up to something bigger, even in small and simple ways?

The Art of Pretending

What's your act that you put on every day?

Perhaps you can get some clues by observing other people's acts. Take the businessperson who declared years ago that she would be president of a big company one day. That requires a suit and briefcase, reading the business section of the paper each morning, and fighting like hell to climb the corporate ladder. To others like her, that "looks good."

Or take the antiestablishment act—the young guy who decides that the conventional route isn't for him and puts on the act of growing a beard, driving an old VW bus, and wearing beat-up jeans. He purposely has no money and goes against the cultural grain whenever he can. To others with the same or similar act, he "looks good."

Then there's the soccer-mom act—someone who is in the social whirl of carpooling kids from one sporting event to the next—or the street-gang act, the yoga-devotee act, or the yoga-teacher act. All of them have accompanying scripts to operate from—ways of communicating both verbally and nonverbally. It's simply a matter of saying, wearing, believing, and doing the right things to keep the performance going.

It's helpful to really take a deep look and get a clear insight into the mask you may be putting on every day. Where are you playing a role and using a predetermined script? And then, consider asking yourself: is this really even *you?*

Come Out from Behind the Script

A lot of us think that if we're really good, organized, educated, and so on, then we'll be in control of how we look. Deep down, we may carry the usual human insecurities of feeling unworthy, unimportant, and unwanted, so we create all kinds of "fix-its" to cover them up. They can include the amassing of degrees, knowledge, wealth, or status to show the outside world that we're worthy. Yes, a lot of those things get us far in life, but underneath them the concern for looking good still has us in its grip. Accomplishment, achievement, and admiration show up as an empty package, because they're coming from a reaction. We're reacting to something on the inside: that little voice of doubt in our head that says we aren't enough of something and that we need the right solution to change it.

Although we're typically unconscious to it, the question *How am I going to get approval?* runs our lives. People even do it in yoga—aiming to do it well, correctly, and intelligently. Take, for example, 32-year-old Amy, who would throw herself full force into mastering anything she took on as a way of compensating for feeling deep down that she wasn't good enough. So of course, she did that on her yoga mat. She practiced daily for years, and when she got to a point where she'd mastered the advanced poses, she actually had a flash of *So what that I've gotten all these poses down? What does it matter?* It was a letdown, since underneath, still, was the feeling that something was wrong and not up to par.

What she discovered was an essential truth of transformation, which is that creating fix-its to cover up our feelings of inadequacy doesn't work. If you're not operating from being and trusting yourself, you'll just keep seeking more solutions, knowledge, skills, stuff, and beliefs that will fix the dilemma—which, in reality, is made up and doesn't exist outside of the mind.

Pretty yoga practices aside, one of the areas where I see my students hide the most is in their speaking. A lot of them will show up to teacher trainings looking for me to give them a script. They want the ABC's of technical knowledge that they can then take home and regurgitate to their own students. They may not realize it, but what they'll get is a script to hide behind so they don't have to be completely out there, exposed in the moment, and teaching from their creative force. To be creative in front of others is to be at risk, and the possibility of failure and looking foolish looms.

One student actually joked, "I'm frustrated, because I know you have 'it,' and I want you to give 'it' to me!" And yeah, she's right, I do have "it," but I have *my* "it"—my own sense of being myself; trusting my inner knowing; and being connected, alive, and creative in the present moment with a roomful of people. It takes a couple of days for students to realize that they're not going to get a cookie-cutter script from me, and this forces them to inquire about what it really means to flow from their own power and sense of self.

Speaking from theory or repeating memorized facts is devoid of energy. There's a huge difference between teaching as a technician versus an artist. One is by rote, the other by strategic intuition and inner direction. When we lack confidence as teachers (and we're all teachers, no matter our walk in life), we tend to use our tool kit of knowledge as a shield: we rely on concepts, facts, learned knowledge, rehearsed speeches, and borrowed quotes.

The problem with going on autopilot is that there's no sense of heart. The zing of realness is missing . . . and is that really fulfilling you? To me, life has fun and spark to it when we're inspired and operating from something deep within. The irony here is that the script that feels so safe as a way to sound brilliant is actually what's keeping us from shining with true brilliance.

Perhaps you don't teach yoga, but consider that you too have scripts you rely on. Most of us are wired up like a jukebox, except in this case it's the world and people around us who put in the quarter and press the button. We automatically react and play the appropriate script to avoid failure in each particular situation. For example, when teaching a yoga class, we might play our "wise and knowledgeable" track; with our boss we may do a number that looks like "Mr. Dependable"; and with members of the opposite sex we choose our "charming and smart" selection.

You want to start listening for those scripts, as they may sound great and make you look good in the eyes of others but aren't powerful because they aren't creative; they're reactive. You might use really nice, smart language, but where are *you?* If someone's talking and everything they're saying is really clever, witty, flowery—too perfect—then there's something missing. They're not sharing of themselves, really, and that's stingy. When you give from your heart with generosity, that kind of expansiveness of being inspires others to align with something bigger within themselves.

Essential Speaking

One of the ways we awaken our power and participate in creating our reality is through what I call *essential speaking*. Essential speaking is about being intentional and communicating straight from the heart. It's the practice of speaking from our own experience and self-discovery rather than from concepts and vague generalities.

Essential language gives voice to our personal experience: speaking from "I" rather than "we," "all of us," or just giving a theoretical overview of a situation. It's far more powerful to speak from "I," because it gives people a sense of *you*.

By their very nature, concepts and descriptions are dry and canned. They're of the head, not the heart. There are two distinct ways to use language, and relaying concepts and theories is much different than sharing directly from your essence. A very spiritual communication between two people is when I have a total experience of you. I can hear your personal reality and what matters to you, not your opinions and descriptions of reality or simply your beliefs. I'm not interested in what you believe; tell me your inner experience. For instance, someone telling me about his or her belief in God isn't very interesting, but an *experience* of God . . . now that holds something for me.

Essential language is transformative and sparks clarity, which generates a new conversation. It moves us from a state of vagueness and detachment (or even helplessness) into taking responsibility for how we're showing up in an actual situation. For example, if people tell you, "My job is a nightmare and stressful," they're describing a scenario in their lives but not really putting themselves inside the experience. If they were to rephrase this using essential language, they might instead say something like, "I am frustrated by my relationship with my boss and don't feel as if I'm being heard." Now we're getting somewhere! Just by making that small shift, you gain access to what's really happening in concrete terms. You then generate an energetic flow and create new possibilities in ways to relate, communicate, and empower yourself now and into a new future. Instead of feeling helpless under the past-based, conceptual, story-land version you've been telling ("It's a nightmare and stressful"), you've taken ownership of the experience and are freed to steer conversations and perceptions in new, energetic directions.

It's the same for listening. Being of power requires that when in a conversation we focus on the experience of each other's essence—the gold—versus the script. Most of us can't really communicate powerfully because we don't typically pay attention to and really get the speaker's experience. Instead, we hear the little know-it-all voice in our head that evaluates the rightness or wrongness of the other person's reality compared with our own. Distinguishing how you listen is the key to evolving the way you communicate. The power of essential speaking is born out of listening from a quiet space in your being.

I'll share a story with you to show you what I mean. One evening in 2003, I was teaching a filled-to-capacity class at my institute in Boston. A few journalists from the local media were doing a story on the popularity of Baptiste Yoga, but they didn't want to participate. They just wanted to observe me teach the class and take notes, so I set up some chairs for them in the back of the room. They were quietly talking amongst themselves as I was simultaneously leading the class, but clearly the conversations were vastly different.

From their seats in the back of the room, the reporters were taking notes about the yoga practice and what people were experiencing on the mat. They were assessing, judging, and making assumptions about what it felt like and describing what certain poses looked like, but they weren't personally engaged in the practice or embodying the experience in a way that gave any access to the benefits of it.

The question this story brings up is this: what type of conversations are you having in your life? Are you on the mat, directing and elevating the energy, expressing from the epicenter of your own experience in ways that inspire creativity, flow, and power? Or are you just observing from the sidelines and *talking* about what's happening around you, not making any real difference?

∞

You know who has the hardest time with essential communication? It's usually those individuals who are highly educated. When you know a lot, you're naturally wired to speak from that base of conceptual knowledge. This was the case with Cynthia, a 22-year-old graduate student who participated in an exercise we do in teacher trainings around "What the training is about." In it, participants write out how they would describe to someone at home what the weeklong transformational training is all about, as if they were talking to someone who had never given personal growth a single thought— a neighbor, for instance. The challenge is to say it in a way that not only makes sense to him, but also to have him walk away feeling as if the transformational results you experienced might be possible for him, too. This doesn't involve convincing anyone or selling it; it's about speaking plainly, concretely, and deeply from the heart without all the window dressing.

Cynthia carefully constructed her piece the way she would a term paper for school and then shared her letter with the group. Here's what she said: "The teacher training program is based on the Baptiste syllabus, which consists of three elements: Baptiste Yoga practice, meditation, and inquiry. As the students move through the seven days, breakthroughs occur as they discover themselves and awaken their inner sense of power."

You could tell that she thought she'd nailed it . . . until the feedback she got from another student was, "That was an A+ paper . . . awesome! You were very thorough in your explanation of what we learned here. But I don't feel you, and I definitely don't know anything about your personal experience, what inspired you, your breakthroughs, or if you had a personal transformation and how that impacted you."

Cynthia realized that she was so wired to present arguments in careful language that she glossed right over what was real and authentic. There was no passion or sense of personal triumph in her words. After a few tries, she whittled her entire essay down to one essential sentence: "Through getting on the mat, meditation, and engaging in a process of self-discovery, I was presented with powerful tools to immediately reestablish vitality and freedom in my body, leaving me with a new inspiration; awareness; and the attitude that I am surrounded with support and can live, breathe, and act from a place of all things being possible in my life."

Bull's-eye! It just clicked with people; you could see it on their faces. This woman had dropped the canned script and spoke from the heart. Essential language can give you that "aha!" It has the kind of dynamic, from-the-heart energy that can make you laugh or cry—it hits a nerve. Sharing from your heart affirms something in you and everyone around you. It affirms something real about humanity and what your life is ultimately for. It takes you over as soon as you express it, and it takes other people over, too. They can see themselves in what you've shared, even if their experience isn't the same as yours.

You want to be someone who reaches through to people, and that doesn't just come automatically. That's the irony here: you actually have to practice being essential, because the world puts so many layers of "should" onto you. That clarity of inspired naturalness is under there, and you just need to uncover it and come out from behind the safety of your protective tool kit and the flowery, vague, story-land language. This kind of articulation starts to roll out a new pathway, and a fresh energy of presence opens up. When you drop your script, you can be intentional, dance with what's right in front of you, and author from your authentic power.

This applies to every area of expression in your life. When you show up and are willing to speak from your heart, come what may, that authenticity communicates directly with other people's hearts. Doing so creates an energy that inspires you and those around you into action. You can transform your entire life with this one simple practice of essential speaking.

———⌘———

PRACTICE #3

GET COMFORTABLE WITH NOT KNOWING

"Live the questions now. Perhaps then, someday far in the future, you will gradually, without even noticing it, live your way into the answer."

— RAINER MARIA RILKE

The global spiritual leader of Tibetan Buddhism, the Dalai Lama, commonly uses the phrase, "I don't know." In his many interviews and public speeches, when asked a question for which he has no answer, with a grin on his face and without apology he will simply reply, "I don't know."

That seems kind of surprising, doesn't it? How can one of the most revered spiritual leaders on the planet not know the answer to something? Even more, how could he be so completely at peace with that?

The Dalai Lama naturally embodies another key tool of transformation, which is to *get comfortable with not knowing.* "I don't know" isn't a stance of ignorance or weakness; actually, it's just the opposite. "I don't know" is powerful, for it's a very high state of learning that allows you to dance with the creative energy of inquiry and self-discovery. When you believe that you already know everything, you're all sewn up, and there's no room for anything new. When we live from inquiry, we open ourselves up and gain access to new ways of seeing.

Giving Up the Need to Know

We all want answers, right? The reason those late-night infomercials are so popular is because everyone wants a fix. Just give us the simple steps, the quick fix, the how-to process. That's how we're conditioned; answers make us feel secure. Whenever we encounter a situation that's uncomfortable for us, we try so hard to figure out how to get through it. Not having a resolution is threatening to us.

Consider for a moment that your need to know is what limits you. There's a big difference between searching for a solution (for example, rushing the process) and living from a state of inquiry and curiosity. Just getting answers is easy. We can go to the Internet and find whatever we need, and the mind likes that. The problem is that we usually stop there. Tell us how to fix it, and then we're done.

Our need to know comes from our desire for control and predictability. We're wired up to play it safe and not fail, and this is what keeps us on a treadmill of collecting answers. We think we'll finally land in some sort of comfort zone if we just figure out how to do things the right way. Not *our* way, not *a* way, but the *right* way. We're absolutely sure that someone else out there knows what it is, and our need to figure it out becomes an addiction. This keeps us squarely in the realm of the head, where our power to create gets squelched and the messages from our own heart get drowned out.

The world conspires in this illusion, because it wants to sell us an answer. We ask "How?" and the world whispers, "This way." We don't trust our own inner knowing, so we live from someone else's advice. The problem is that their solution came out of their experience, not our own. Sure, their opinions and ideas might be helpful or even empowering, but in the big picture, how fulfilling is it to live based on someone else's answers?

The other issue with getting answers in this way is that this supposed fixed knowledge becomes a sort of lens through which you relate to your situation. Perhaps it works for a while, but life isn't static, and neither are you. At a certain point, what works for you changes. You know how it's been said that you can never step into the same river twice because the water is always flowing? Well, it's the same with life. It's malleable, always moving, and forever changing. The knowledge and insight you get today may be really useful, and may even lead to a huge breakthrough. But by tomorrow, it's yesterday's news, because each day you awaken standing in a new river.

So let's say that you get an answer to something you've been stuck on. A powerful practice is to pause there, open your eyes, and be willing to look beyond the answer into what you have not yet seen. Can you temporarily put it on a shelf and keep going into "I don't know what else it is that I don't know or see" and live in the realm of inquiry? This is a practice of being a yes: interested, curious, and open to discovering yourself and whatever lies beyond the obvious.

We start to get comfortable with not knowing when we remove the idea that there's something wrong with it. We rush to get to conclusions, because we're programmed to view uncertainty as a problem. Yet an artist doesn't view a blank canvas as a crisis; she sees limitless creative possibility in it. Raw possibility is something we can feel. It's actually kind of cool when we can experience it in that way, rather than it being something to panic about. Huge opportunities are lost when we rush to fill this fertile, empty space.

Often our need to know shows up as a question of *how*. That's what people in my trainings always seem to want to know: *how* do I have a breakthrough, *how do* I do the poses right, *how do* I lead the right way, *how do* I get unstuck, *how do* I fix the situation that is causing me to struggle. When we're stuck in the question of "how," we are expressing doubt in ourselves and our intuitive power to create. It's as if we're mechanics who lack the right tool to get the job done.

This is not an argument against learning how to do something, which can, of course, be helpful, necessary, and even important. Rather, it raises the possibility that there are more expansive questions from which to generate growth. Consider that how to do it right, how to fix it, how to solve it, how to do it better, and so on should be asked later rather than sooner. We can be so quick to get practical right away that we create limitations on what we might discover if we ask instead, "What is possible?" We diminish ourselves to being overly pragmatic and technical, as the artist and visionary in us gets lost.

A New Way of Listening

Marcus was a dynamic, funny guy who came to a workshop feeling stuck and struggling in most areas of his life. He was especially ready to have a breakthrough in his way of relating to the people close to him, wanting to feel more connected. Throughout the week, he generously shared with other participants the insights he was getting from the program about how he could do that.

At one point, Marcus came up to the microphone and waited patiently (or so it seemed) while the person in front of him finished speaking. Then he took the mic and said, "You know, I was going to share something completely different than what I'm about to say. Because I just realized about 45 seconds ago that as present as I think I am, I spent the entire time up here rehearsing in my head what I was going to talk about. I didn't hear a word that anyone else shared, and that's pretty much exactly what I do all the time at home and with everyone in my life."

I acknowledged Marcus for his capacity to listen to *how* and *from where* he was listening and his ability to distinguish the voice in his head from what he was actually hearing other people say. That was a true breakthrough in relating to others.

I then asked Marcus if he finds that people generally don't listen to him, and if he was often left feeling unheard in his relationships. He responded with an astounding, "Yes! My wife doesn't listen to me, and neither does my family. It's as if I'm never heard or understood." I offered him a tip: "You want to focus on being really committed to paying attention to others. Start getting interested in what your friends and family members are saying—really engage—and you'll see that this will shape how they focus on you when you speak."

Transformation occurs by shifting how you listen. When you do so from a space of genuine curiosity and get interested in what others have to say, you create the possibility of deep connection. Listening from "I don't know" rather than "I already know" opens up that same new space of discovery. You already know and have all the stuff that's in your head . . . what else might be available to you by moving beyond that?

✌

There's a very funny recording made by the Indian meditation teacher Osho about how the word *fuck* has replaced *God* in our language as the universal word of choice. One of the participants, Nancy, had heard the recording at her first training course with me and was laughing so hard that tears were streaming down her face.

Well, Nancy ended up taking the course a second time, and when we got to this part her brain immediately went to, "Oh . . . I know this recording. I know what's coming. I thought it was hilarious the first time I heard it, too." Her listening was constrained by a "been there, done that" filter, which took her out of the present experience.

So while 150 other participants were cracking up, Nancy just kind of sat there, feeling a little smug. And then, as the group kept on laughing, she saw what she'd done. She'd been so caught up in what she'd already experienced that she didn't allow for the possibility that something would strike her in a new way this time. Her way of listening had closed her off from experiencing something fresh in the present moment.

I know that most of you reading this already know a great deal. The good news is that you get to keep all the knowledge and insight you already have. And that's awesome. But listening for what you don't already know will give you access to something new.

Consider that maybe, like Marcus, the opportunities for growth aren't inside your head, but in your ability to hear others and distinguish what will empower rather than mentally writing your script while waiting for your turn to talk. Listen from a space of, "I am expanding my awareness and getting a deeper sense of this person. I suspend what I know and step fully into what she's sharing to see what it sparks in me."

When we drop our judgments about whether what they're saying is right or wrong or if we agree or disagree and just listen with curiosity, we can see ourselves in other people's experiences. Intentional listening from the heart enables us to create space and experience new possibilities and growth for our own lives.

Who Are You?

You know who you are, right? But think about it for a moment . . . do you really? Consider that you don't know everything that's available for you to know about who you are. That's good news, because it puts you on a path of discovery.

Whether you're conscious of it or not, you most likely cling to your sense of who you are. There's a good chance that you identify with the accomplishments and achievements that it has brought you. You're not just a lawyer, mom, student, or whatever. Yes, they may be accurate labels to describe roles that you play, but they don't answer the question, *Who are you?* Those are layers of "not us" that obscure who we really are underneath.

We don't actually "figure out" who we are. That's just another quest for finite answers. We get to it by giving up the "not us." We start peeling the onion, layer by layer, letting go of the layers of adopted identity: all the people pleasing, the roles we've taken on to make sure we look good, and the scripts we've been using. We begin to see the areas where we've adopted or inherited those ideas about who we should and shouldn't be in order to fit in and adapt to our environment. This is an inquiry about giving up the false sense of self—which has been in the driver's seat of our lives—and identifying what's most important to us and getting in alignment with what's in our hearts. Giving up the "not us" is the process and the path, and it all starts with accepting that we may not really know who we are just yet.

When we shed a layer of who we've been pretending to be, we don't know who the new us is yet. Standing in that new, exposed space, without the security of what we believed to be true about ourselves, can be extremely uncomfortable. Often, our first instinct is to run back to the safety of our old ways.

I'll never forget this story that a student named Taylor shared. Taylor made some mistakes when he was in his early 20s, and as a result served three years in a federal prison. On the day he was released, he stood outside the prison door, terrified to walk the 100 yards to the fence that stood between him and the outside world. He knew there was a new life waiting for him on the other side, but emotionally, all he wanted to do was turn around and go back to the comfort of the reality he'd known for a good part of his young life. Imagine choosing the hell of prison over the freedom to create your life. It's something a lot of us do, even when there aren't any iron bars.

Taylor didn't know what was on the other side for him. Standing there in that yard, he was right on the edge between his comfort zone and the realm of pure possibility. Every time we peel back a layer, we stand at that same edge. The right question is not, "Will I survive if I step out of my comfort zone?" but rather, "Will I survive my comfort zone?" Transformation happens right in those moments when rather than running back to our self-created prisons, we embrace the unknown and ask ourselves, "What's available to me from here?"

The Ongoing Practice

Any student who has taken a Baptiste Yoga class, workshop, or bootcamp has been reminded that it's not called a yoga *perfect,* it's a yoga *practice.* There's no end goal in and of itself, but when we get intentional and committed to creating the bigger-picture results that we want (transforming fear, pain, and stress into strength, vitality, and confidence), then breakthroughs happen. The results come from showing up; doing the work; and going past those physical and attitudinal edges where you'd rather flee than stay, breathe, and move forward.

Inquiry is also an ongoing practice throughout our lives. Transformation isn't something that happens once and then we're done; it's a lifelong path of self-renewal and taking responsibility for ourselves. It takes humility to realize that yesterday's transformation is today's ego trip.

We want to give up the idea that we've already done the work—that we've "arrived." Mr. Iyengar used to say, "The minute you think you've arrived, you get squashed like a bug." When we get all filled up with knowledge and accomplishment, we become proud. There's a kind of righteousness that we can get, because it gives us a sense of being more advanced than others. There's a lot of that in the yoga world—people thinking that they're more enlightened yogis because they can do handstands or they're super bendy or more evolved than others because they meditate every day.

So there we are, thinking we've arrived and feeling pretty proud of ourselves . . . and then *bam!* The universe comes along and delivers a fist right to the belly, just to remind us that our journey is not finished—that we still have blind spots and there is more room to grow. I've reached points in my life where I thought I had things all figured out, only to be taken out by a sucker punch from the universe. My knees have hit the ground and I've landed in the emotional fetal position on many occasions, but each time has been a great source of learning for me. In those moments when I gave up the righteousness and asked, "What am I not seeing that I need to see?" I discovered powerful lessons that turned the breakdowns into breakthroughs. I saw how humility is a key tool when we hit bottom, that there's a kind of surrender to a higher power that comes from giving up our insistence to do it our way.

What I am saying here is not to diminish or take away from all of the personal development you have done. At this point in your life, you've probably amassed an immense amount of answers, knowledge, and wisdom. Maybe you've immersed yourself in growth work, vision questing, prayer, and practices such as yoga and meditation. You've been mentored, coached, taught, and been a teacher and coach to others. But what you've done in the past, no matter how beneficial, is in the past. You've got to let go of that and create a space for the new growth, but thoughts such as, *I already did that, I already figured that out,* or *I already got what I needed from this* don't allow for real depth and mastery.

Rather than thinking you're already evolved enough because you've done all this work, you can take the position of, "Yeah, I've done work to a certain level, but there's always the next transformation that's looking for me and another possibility that wants me." In my experience, learning and discovery never end. Every new level is a new view. Yours up until now may have been from one side of the mountain, but there's always another vantage point from which to create anew. Call yourself out whenever you start slipping into believing that you've arrived, because it's a crock. If you want to be of power, you'll need to keep shifting your vision to the next level and maintain an open inquiry of "I know that I don't know" and "I don't know what I don't know."

The most empowered place we can be is not, "I've got it all figured out." It's to be brave enough to ask the questions over and over, "What am I not seeing that's limiting me? What do I need to see that's new for me?" We're afraid to ask that, because we're worried about what we might have to confront and deal with as a result. But that's what frees us: facing what we need to face, giving up what we need to give up, and being a yes for what's next.

So can you get comfortable with the idea that you haven't "arrived" yet? Can you give up your need to know what's next and just get curious, be in inquiry, and open to a breakthrough even if you don't know what it is at this point?

———— ∽ ————

GIVE IT UP TO GET EMPTY

*"The winds of grace are blowing all the time;
you have only to raise your sail."*

— RAMAKRISHNA

I once heard a story about how Michelangelo supposedly used to walk through the streets of Florence carrying a slab of uncut marble on his back, saying, "There is an angel inside here screaming to get out." This masterful artist didn't just see a big piece of uncut stone. Rather, he saw the statue he would create as already hidden inside the marble, and his job was to chisel away all the excess so it could be revealed.

It's the same for us as human beings. We're already whole, complete, and lacking nothing; the problem is that, for the most part, we don't believe this about ourselves. Since we were very young, many of us have adopted the belief that being ourselves is not enough, and from there we added on all the fix-its in an attempt to navigate a world where we are not enough, we want to please others, and we receive the admiration and acknowledgment that we're craving. We've obscured our true selves and thus lost our power. Our work here in this practice is to break off the excess marble that keeps our authentic, whole selves encumbered.

We hear a lot in the spiritual and self-help world about the idea of letting go. That's pretty common these days, right? I mean, how many yoga teachers have a bumper sticker or T-shirt that says something along the lines of LET GO? We all know that there's something philosophical to that notion. In reality, though, beyond just being a nice sound bite, letting go is a key tool to rediscovering your power. Being of power is all about coming back to our naturalness—it's clearing the clutter that's preventing us from tapping into what's possible.

Our higher self is not something we have to go out and seek. Over the years, I've met many individuals who have tried to turn yoga into "the path"—those who seek out one guru, teacher, or workshop after another or journey far and wide looking for enlightenment. But maybe there really isn't some higher self that you need to find somewhere in India or the Himalayas. Consider that you already have it right now, that you were born with it. It's right here, in you, waiting for you to wake up to it. To be about what you really want in life, in your heart of hearts, you only need to give up whatever is standing in your way.

I'm reminded of a lesson I learned when I was 18 years old. I was traveling with my parents to Myanmar (formerly called Burma) on one of their pilgrimages to the East. We visited a very old Buddhist monastery where we met with a group of monks, and my dad was introduced to the head monk as "a famous guru from America." After a few minutes of polite chitchat, the monks wanted to test my father to find out if he was for real. "It's customary," our guide explained, so Dad agreed.

The master handed him a small, ancient bowl with Buddhist symbols painted all over it and asked, "What is the most important part of this bowl?" I remember that there was this kind of macho-monk energy exchange going on as we all waited in anticipation for my father to give his answer.

He looked over the bowl as if he were keenly interested in the symbols painted on it, the texture, and the shape. Finally, after a long pause, he answered, "The space inside." It was the right answer. The energy in the room lightened, and everyone started laughing. My father and the Buddhist master instantly got on as if they were old friends.

When I train people, I work a lot with the fundamental idea of space, which is the "rice bowl" in which personal transformation happens. One of the barriers we typically bump up against when we're trying to forge a new direction in life is occupied space. We try to do something new without first making room for it. The problem with this is that we can't build anything new on top of old, stuck energy. That would be like trying to erect a new building on top of an existing one; it simply won't work. So before we can move forward to create the life we want, we first have to clear out whatever debris of the past might be cluttering our space. This chapter helps us do exactly that.

Removing the Bricks

Eric came to a training that I was leading looking for a spiritual and physical renovation and renewal. He explained that he imagined his entire life as a building that needed to be torn down, piece by piece. He wanted to "break down the walls and flatten it all to the ground," and I told him that this particular imagery works well.

I will refer here to the things we need to let go of as bricks. We carry around these heavy blocks of disempowering beliefs, fear, resentment, expectation, resignation, cynicism, and blame, to name a few, so it's no wonder people feel so exhausted and burned out!

Giving things up is a health secret. One by one, brick by brick, when we drop the heavy bricks that have been weighing us down, we immediately feel more energized. We lighten up and even begin to *look* that way. You can actually see the difference between people's energy when they arrive at a Baptiste training program versus when they leave. Typically, they come in with dense, stressed, resistant energy that had been building up from years of living a reactive existence. But then somewhere around day three, this embodied resistance and heaviness starts breaking up, participants start breaking through into a new lightness of being, and everything about them changes. Their eyes start to shine and they stand taller, get a bounce back in their step, and start to glow with an inner brightness. It's like a total mind-body makeover, but from the inside out. The breakthroughs happen when they shift from asking what they need to *do* to the question of what they need to *give up*.

When students feel stuck, I usually ask them, "What do you need to give up right now to be at peace?" Not surprisingly, one of the most common answers is, "Fear."

Veronica, a 35-year-old executive, once shared these comments at a workshop: "My whole life I've been held back by fear. I'm afraid of what people think, afraid of failing, afraid of succeeding . . . afraid of everything. But then, this morning during meditation, I realized that when it comes to ability and opportunity, there's actually nothing real standing in my way. I'm smart, educated, and fortunate to have a good life and a solid support system around me. So, really, all things are possible in my life—fear is the only thing in my way."

Veronica is right. We can't be of possibility and run our fear-based story lines at the same time. The limiting perceptions born out of fear keep us from finding love, acting on our dreams, and succeeding in taking on and accomplishing the aspirations that ultimately fulfill us. It pretty much follows that whenever we feel stopped, fear is at play.

Just imagine for a moment what your life would be like if you could transform fear into faith-filled action every time it comes up . . . what you could be and do if that brick wasn't weighing you down. It's a pretty empowering possibility, isn't it?

Another big brick we carry is expectation. In any circumstance where we feel frustration, this is usually at play. Expectations rob us of a sense of peace in the present moment, because they keep us in the divide between what is actually happening now and what we believe should be taking place. Take Sid, for example. He is a Christian minister who came to a teacher training because he loves Baptiste Yoga and wanted to advance in his own practice but not necessarily teach it. Well, not a lot was going right for Sid as the week began. On day one he pulled a muscle, and for the next few days he was frustrated because he couldn't physically work at the level he wanted.

I explained to Sid that while his physical pain is real and needs to be respected, it was important to distinguish that from his *mental reaction and emotional experience of the injury.* What was causing him to suffer was his pre-sumption that his body should perform differently than it actually was.

Dropping the expectation, as in giving up the brick called *this should not be happening this way,* shifts us into a more empowered space of equanimity and acceptance rather than frustration. You can simply be with what is just as it is, without having to make anything wrong with it, and new, unexpected opportunities for action will occur. We'll talk about this more in "Practice #7: Embrace Naked Reality," but for now we must consider that our expectations (and subsequent frustrations) prevent us from gleaning what's available on the actual path that's unfolding right before our eyes.

There are plenty of other bricks that we human beings carry around. Start looking for the ones of heavy seriousness and significance that you bring to nearly everything in your life—including your yoga practice, if you have one. Root out the goal-driven, get-it-right, be-right, and do-it-perfectly-or-not-at-all attitude and give that up, because it's a pure killjoy. Give all that up in order to lighten up. Stop making such a big deal out of things. Relax already! Stop taking things personally, because they aren't.

As you drop these heavy bricks, you become one of life's players in bringing lightness, fun, joy, and ease into everything you do.

ᕲ

We give something up, moment by moment as it arises, through three steps:

1. Awareness

2. Acceptance

3. Declaration

Let's say fear shows up a lot for you. You can alleviate its effects by doing the following:

— The first step is to become *aware* that fear is present. Each time you do so, it's an opportunity to give it up. Right in that moment, you can choose with a clear perspective whether to continue to let fear control you or to drop it.

I'm not talking about resisting, since what we resist we empower. The more powerful path is to acknowledge it, feel it, let it come up, and let it go. Remember, when we're not paying attention to fear in this way, it has us in its grip—it's driving the bus. But when we're aware of it, we can choose whether to give it control or take back the steering wheel.

— The second step is *acceptance*. It's the action of embracing the fear as it is and as it isn't and giving up any of the resistance to what you see and feel. You give up judging what is bad or good, right or wrong, and release any fault, blame, or whatever other story you're spinning about it ("This shouldn't be happening," "I don't want this," and so on).

We'll deepen our exploration of this in "Practice #5: Let it Be," but this is a good place to start.

— The third step, *declaration,* is exactly what it sounds like. You simply—but intentionally—declare, "Right now, I give up fear." Note that I didn't say, "I'm going to give up fear," "I'll try my best to give up fear," or "I want to give up fear." There is immeasurable power in declaration that works if we own it in the present *as if it's already real, true, and in existence.* The amazing thing is that you don't even need to believe it's true in the moment. Just the act of declaring in words, silently or aloud, sets the intent energetically in motion and primes the space to bring that thing into existence. It also puts our attention on what we want to have happen and takes our intention off what's stopping us.

This isn't magic. It's a practice. We don't declare something once and then *boom!* we're done. A student named Donna had a deep fear of speaking in front of big groups, but she desperately wanted to be a leader for change in her community. She was very clear that it was fear standing in her way—specifically, a fear of how people would perceive her—so on day one of her training she got up and declared that she was giving up the brick of fear. And then she immediately said, "Hmm . . . but the fear is still here."

It's like that, right? You give something up, and then it just slithers right back in. The voice of the inner saboteur in your head says, "That's a crock . . . you're full of it." Well, it's important to understand that it's not an instantaneous transformation here! Just let that voice be, and give up the brick called fear, again and again, in every moment. When you give it up and it comes back, acknowledge it, feel it, and simply give it up again. Take every opportunity to release it.

If you have an apprehension of speaking in front of groups, for instance, every time someone asks you to do it, acknowledge the fear, give it up, and stand up to openly share from your heart. Repetition is the mother of mastery until ease and confidence crystallize as something real and permanent in your way of being. Acting courageously doesn't happen in the absence of fear, but rather in the face of it. As you learn to dance with this emotion in a more playful way, notice how it loses its strength. The impermanence of fear becomes obvious when we get present to it.

This isn't just a simple, "Oh, give it up." It's not a gloss over. People will oftentimes tell others who are going through something difficult—like heartbreak, for example—that they should let go and move on. But on some level, the individuals who are saying that know it doesn't really work, even for them. You can't really give anything up or let it go until you've taken ownership of the experience of it in the first place. Just let the feeling or thought be there, and then in the moment of distinguishing it as something separate from you, put some space between you and the experience. From this context, you're no longer consumed by the fear or heartbreak or whatever else is causing you a loss of peace. Its grip on you is released. You can't give up the heartbreak if you're caught up in the story about it, but you can give up your *resistance* to the heartbreak and take ownership for what's underneath. You can give up the brick of "this should not be happening," accept that it happened, and feel what you're feeling with the intent to heal and get whole. As Robert Frost said, "The best way out is always through."

This is how we give up and go beyond whatever it is that's standing in the way of our being of power. Moment by moment, brick by brick: awareness, acceptance, declaration.

So what do you need to give up right now to be a new kind of power?

Clearing Your Space

I love the physical focus of yoga. The emphasis on getting grounded and tuned in to our bodies is an access point to our power. Asana practice is a waking up and energetic clearing out that directly connects us to our bodies, which is the space in which we exist in every present moment. It helps us remove the blocks and trapped energy we store there, sometimes for years or even decades. Giving up and dissolving old energy patterns allows us to empty our rice bowl, which clears the space and allows us to listen from our body intelligence and take intuitive, decisive action.

The three practices and techniques of Baptiste transformative methodology are physical asana, meditation, and inquiry. Meditation, as I teach it, is a body-based observation practice. You can accomplish a lot by taking ten minutes in the morning and evening to energetically go through your space (your body) and check in, scan, and create a clearing of good space.

The following is a meditation exercise I use that you can do on your own at home. I suggest having someone else read this to you, or record yourself reading it and play it back:

— Choose a seated position in a place that feels comfortable to you. Lift your bones and relax your muscles in a way that is empowering to you. Close your eyes, and let your arms hang loosely as you rest your hands on your lap. Relax your entire body with the intention of checking in and getting a sense of your physical space.

— Start by giving attention to the physical space you are sitting in. Sense the earth or floor beneath you, the sky or ceiling above you, and the natural environment or four walls around you. Notice your body occupying physical space in relation to all those elements.

— Move your attention to your inner space. Get a sense of your spine and bones as the support structure for your body and of your skin as the container for its contents.

— Now, funnel your awareness into your hands, and feel what's going on inside of them at this moment. Notice how where your focus goes your energy flows. Continue to scan your arms, then move up to your shoulders, neck, and head. Imagine that your attention is a warm, thick, glowing, golden liquid, and let it pour down from the top of your head into your torso, arms, pelvis, buttocks, thighs, calves, ankles, and feet. Just be with the sensations inside your body, and check in with what's happening inside your space. Imagine yourself as a magnet, open to receiving a flush of warmth through-out your space as you do your scan. It's okay if you don't feel the energy flowing through you at first—don't get caught up in evaluating what you feel, see, and sense or the running mental commentary about it. Don't make anything bad or wrong; just feel whatever you feel and experience whatever you experience while staying aware and inside your physical space.

Don't worry about the specific position or condition of your body. Just be here, inside your space, looking around. Look at any mental images that happen to arise, and let them pass by and move through. Whatever feelings or thoughts come up, let them, and then let them go. Move your attention into your organs—your heart, lungs, and abdomen. Scan your whole inner space, top to bottom, bottom to top, from your toes to your temples, from your skin to your bones.

— Now move your awareness up to your head, and just notice what's there. Is there a quality of spaciousness or contraction? Take a look at the area behind your eyes and around your brain. As you breathe and scan, let any sense of tightness or clutter in your brain, skull, eyes, or jaw muscles dissolve like an ice cube in hot water. Just breathe, experience, let be, and relax.

If you locate aches, pains, tightness, or fatigue anywhere, look at these things up close. Specifically, locate the feelings of stuck energy and resistance in your body. Move your attention exactly to where the tension, discomfort, or sensation of tiredness exists. Where exactly is it? How big is it—the size of a grape, grapefruit, or watermelon? How far in is it? What color does it have? What is its texture? Is it moving or static? Are there any thoughts, judgments, or images from your past that are attached to it? Just notice what's there without trying to change it; simply watch and be with it.

— Next, imagine your body as a clear glass container that's filled in every nook and cranny with warm, golden, liquid sunshine. Notice the quality of inner brightness that this liquid carries as it fills your feet, calves, thighs, pelvis, torso, and arms and continues to move up steadily all the way to the top of your head.

— Now visualize that each of your ten toes and fingers has a release valve at its tip. Open these valves, and let the warm liquid begin to drain slowly out of you. Feel it draining downward from your head and neck and through the rest of your body, cleansing your space. As the substance drains out of your body, imagine it having a spongelike quality that allows it to absorb and soak up any resistance, toxic energy, tension, judgments, negative beliefs, and other junk that has been polluting your space and making it heavy. Remember the intention here is to clear and unclutter your energetic space. Let every last drop of the warm liquid release out of you.

— To complete the exercise, once more do a body scan and look around inside, noticing how you've cleared your space. If you notice any remaining holding patterns, just let them be. Breathe deeply and enjoy the sensation of a fulfilling, healthy emptiness. For these last few moments, imagine a flame near your heart igniting a glowing brightness that streams throughout your inner space and infuses every part of your body with the energy of pure possibility.

— You can open your eyes now and stretch.

As you get more connected to your space, you'll be amazed by the feedback and messages you receive about what you're doing in your life that's working, what isn't, and the old stuff you may be carrying around that's weighing you down.

At one of my programs, a student named Bill described to the group how in his life he had faced a lot of challenges. Most recently, he'd been struggling with depression. He shared that, through his scanning meditation practice, he got in touch with a body sensation of coldness that had been present for a long time, and he began to shiver. A powerful image came to mind of himself as a five-year-old boy in Philadelphia on a day when it had snowed. He was playing outside, when he suddenly got very cold and passed out on the sidewalk. He remembered experiencing a tremendous fear of being left alone, which has haunted him ever since.

Bill told us, "I realized that this cold, deadened sensation has always been there in the background for me. So I tuned in to where it was showing up in my body—specifically, it was my belly. Up until then, I always thought it had been a problem in my body, but I suddenly realized that the feeling wasn't physical at all. It was fear. So I kept going, tuning in deeper, to see if I could figure out what I was actually scared of. The answer came really quickly: I was afraid of being left alone to die."

Even through years of therapy, Bill hadn't gotten in touch with the loneliness that was so dominant in his life, because he'd always resisted it. He told us that after fully experiencing the feeling of aloneness, the cold lifted, and he felt greatly relieved. The chill was replaced by a flush of warmth throughout his body, as he realized that being alone is different from being lonely. He saw how he'd been adding a lot of negative meaning to both, but due to the internal work he did, the coldness subsequently dissolved permanently.

It's helpful to discern why body patterns such as Bill's persist. Often, there's a hidden energy and emotion underneath the symptom or sensation that keeps it in place, even when the person wishes for it to change. Bill was only able to let it go once the concealed feeling came to light. Only then did the pattern lose its hold over him and new energy was freed up in his body.

When we scan our space, unconscious blind spots come to view. We see mental dynamics that have had us in their grip, and they begin to dissolve as we practice working with them in a new way. Those who ignore the sensations and feelings inside their bodies miss out on the possibility of experiencing deeper personal insights regarding whatever has happened that caused those dynamics—and thus being able to release old patterns and come into new vitality and freedom. From this open space, we have direct access to our higher intuition and spiritual gut sense, which comes from the core of who we are. That's our authentic power, right there, waiting for us to wake up to it.

Create Space for Grace

Jeremy was entirely sure his mother had taught him how to walk when he was a small child. He was convinced that if it weren't for her, he wouldn't have attained that skill as a toddler. I told Jeremy I fully understood that he thought his mother had taught him how to walk, and I believed that she held his hand and explained things to him along the way—but, in fact, she did not teach him how to walk. Instead, as a young child, he had expanded his space to include the possibility of walking, and then progressively filled in that space with steps until he fully walked. Mostly, his mother just got to observe and support the process.

I pointed out to Jeremy that if people really needed to be taught how to walk, there would be books like *How to Teach Your Child to Walk* and *Walking for Dummies* on the shelves of bookstores. But there aren't. Children who are ready to walk simply do it. As a parent, you can help the process along, but you can't speed it up or slow it down—not really.

Today, as adults, this is how we acquire new skills. Our space is where we're coming from, and our purpose—our goals—is where we're going. Just as when we learned to walk, the only things we can ever do in life are the things we expand our space to include. Today, just as when we were kids, we have the ability to know intuitively if we can do something. And I mean really *know*. And then from that inner knowing, we just go ahead and do it.

Think about it: was there anything in your life that you just knew you could do? Maybe it was something creative, brave, or physical, and even if you didn't have the technical knowledge just yet at that point, you knew deep inside that you could take it on.

This inner knowing is generated when you're coming from a clear space, because it creates room for grace to enter. When life supports our efforts and paves the way for us so we can move effortlessly ahead, that is grace.

The biggest breakthroughs, awakenings, support, and results that come your way are through grace. The practices you're learning here create the space for these types of expansive manifestations to occur. Clearing the old stuff out to make room for grace means that you're willing to be the recipient of a gift. To be really open to all that life wants to give you is to come from a place where you fully embrace your self-worth—even if you don't just yet. When you believe that you're not enough, you'll struggle with being receptive to something that you don't feel you deserve. If you experience being unworthy, you won't be able to accept life's abundance—you'll be blocked from receiving miracles.

Consider that if you don't feel this abundance and support from grace, it's because you're not living these practices that serve your transformation. You're being a "no," needing to know "how," having to be right, looking good, and having to do things the "right way" or *your* way (which is all about trying to control circumstances). One way of being is about reaction and survival, the other is about trust and possibility. With the first one, you're working so hard to survive something, and there's no space within the knots of that struggle for grace to come in and support you. If miracles aren't happening, consider that it's because somewhere in there you're playing God and, therefore, grace—the universe—can't get to you. *Giving it up to get empty* is actually a beautiful practice, because it allows us to let go of all the limiting perceptions and stuck energy and be malleable, willing recipients of the gifts of grace.

Clarity of Intent

Remember how I said that you can look at something and know if you can or can't do it? A simple example is looking at a door and knowing whether or not you can walk through it. Can you get to it? Does it open? Assuming it's physically possible, if you declare to yourself, "I can," then it's as if you've already done it. In your being, it's okay to go ahead and walk through the door. You don't have any doubts or obstructions standing in your way.

It's the same with any intention you set for yourself in life. Once you clear your space, your aspirations become easier to reach, since you'll know right away if something is attempting to distract or derail you. I remember receiving a phone call a few years ago informing me that my son had been injured playing football. He was only 11 years old, and it was a bad injury; his lip had been torn, and he was in the hospital needing stitches. I recall the sensation of immediately expanding my space to look ahead, get out the door, and dart directly to the emergency room. In my mind, I was there with him already. There were no reasons or excuses why I couldn't get to the hospital. With the clear purpose of getting to my son, nothing and no one could have gotten in my way. I remember getting there with a lightness of speed and moving through any blocks on my path with ease.

That's the power of intent. If you connect clearly to the things you know you can have and want, then you'll find that the actual process of doing them is an effortless flow. Intention gives us new vision, in which suddenly things that seemed impossible appear as possible. Having a focused intent is what will enable you to give up what stands in your way. It's not magic; you have to take the steps, use the tools, and do the work. But you've cleared the space and invited in grace, which, when present, gains you access to the realm of transformative possibility.

We need to repeatedly come back to the fundamental practice of giving things up to get empty. (A physical reminder I use is to focus on my hands and visualize: with one hand I clear space and allow creative energy to enter into it, and with the other hand I create fulfillment.) Whenever you feel stuck, are unsure about what steps to take, or are ready for something bigger in your life, the question to always begin with is, "What do I need to give up right now?"

The mind always clings, but we increase our power and freedom when we drop the clinging. Each day is new; each *moment* is new. Each day we move into a new world, either dragging the past with us or letting it go to attract and act in ways that fulfill our higher commitments. If we give up the barriers and pretenses and bring into view the things that we weren't aware of about ourselves, take responsibility for them, and clear them, what we have underneath is love. Love is what's left when we get all the other junk out of the way. In the space of love, all things are possible.

———⸉⸜———

LET IT BE

"Power is the ability to be and let be."
— ARISTOTLE

There is nothing you need to change.
There is nothing you need to fix.
There is nothing you need to figure out.

If you're anything like the thousands of students who have stared blankly at me when I've said those words, you're probably wondering how you're supposed to evolve if I'm telling you that there's nothing you need to fix. I mean, you're here to transform, so why would I be saying that there's nothing you need to change?

Here's why: because there is a fundamental difference between *changing form* and *total regeneration.* We always want to fix something outside ourselves, rearrange the pieces, repair whatever we think is "wrong." We can change jobs, relationships, cities, and circumstances. And yes, maybe for a while that gives us some relief. But no matter what we do, where we move, or who we're in a relationship with, changing the form of something is temporary, and fix-its never work in the long term (as we already know). Unless we transform our way of being from the inside out, it all ends up being and feeling the same, because we're still showing up with the same mind-set. As Albert Einstein said, "We can't solve problems by using the same kind of thinking we used when we created them."

When I was in my 20s, I went through a period where I was working around the clock and feeling pretty burned out. I was teaching 22 wall-to-wall, packed group classes a week in Los Angeles, plus dozens more private sessions. At one point, I went to Hawaii to rejuvenate. I traveled thousands of miles, arrived on my favorite island of Kauai, and went down to the beach. I sat there on the beautiful, white sand, taking it all in: the crystalline blue ocean and the perfume of the fragrant flowers all around me. *Now,* I thought, *I'll find some peace.*

It was paradise . . . but there was only one problem. I was there. My surroundings had changed, but all the heaviness in my head, heart, and body had come right along with me. It was then that I realized the profundity of the Zen saying, "No matter where you go, there you are." We're always seeking something outside that will help reinspire us, but going to work on our circumstances is rarely the answer. The only shift that can awaken and renew us is the one that comes from the transformation of our inner substance.

If you took a banana and turned it into a mango, that wouldn't be transformation—it would be a change of form. But if you took a banana and turned it into a banana that tasted like a mango, that would be transformation, because the new fruit would look the same but possess entirely new qualities. Transformation means housing a different quality and substance inside the same form.

When you undergo a transformation, the world is unchanged. Your environment, situation, and immediate circumstances are all the same. How you feel, see, listen, think, and act are what have been altered, and who you are and how you relate to the individuals and things in your life is what shifts. Imagine feeling completely renewed, *without having to change a single thing about your physical reality.* The beautiful thing here is that by transforming the way you relate to life, circumstances around you will ultimately shift as well.

The Myth of Solutions

You want to give up the idea that you can figure out how to solve any of the problems in your life, because I promise that you can't. If you could figure everything out, you would have by now. As they say in 12-step programs, your very best, smartest thinking led you to where you are right now. Thinking your way out isn't the answer.

Trying doesn't work, either. We already know that there is no such thing as "try"; there is only "do." Trying to lose 20 pounds doesn't mean anything. It's actually doing the work necessary to drop the weight that matters. So you can stop trying, too.

Oh, and while you're at it, you can also stop "having faith." That's not what this conversation is about, because people turn that into expecting miracles and believing that magic will take over. You'll probably be waiting for a long time, if not forever.

But this reality is far from hopeless. It's actually good news when we finally understand that we don't have to fight to overcome anything. We don't have to fix our problems; that's just more change. Rather, we want to re-create our perceptions of them. We don't get "unstuck." We come into our authenticity, and then the stuck energy melts away. Jesus, one of the greatest teachers who ever lived, said, "The truth shall set you free." Notice that he didn't say, "Face the truth, and then go fix it."

From my own experience, what I can humbly add is that owning the truth reveals who you *really* are. You shift from within, and then, from real power, are able to let go of everything that isn't you (the excess marble, if you will). Suddenly you'll see previously obscured pathways that are now available to you.

This may sound like bad news to any of you type A personalities out there who want a clear-cut agenda, but there is no "how" when it comes to getting to your authenticity. Thinking, trying, or hoping your way into being real won't work. As I've said, we don't need to fix, figure out, or do anything. There is *no thing* to do. The truth is right here, fully available to us in every single present moment. All we need to do is open up to it, let it in, experience it, and let it be.

What You Embrace Dissolves

We have a slogan in the Baptiste program, which is, "Come into practice as you are, not as you think you should be." People show up to my courses thinking that they should have been doing a lot more practice, be in better shape, have more experience with yoga or transformational work, or whatever. But the training wouldn't have been any better or more powerful for them if they'd done all those things; it just would have been different.

As we talked about in "Practice #4: Give It Up to Get Empty," the key is to work with what you have going on in your body, mind, and life right now. When we focus on what's happening, and not what we think should be, we gain access to the power and possibility of the present moment.

We all face a paradox. In order to grow, we need to start from total acceptance of where we are and where we're not, what we have and what's missing—*exactly as it is*. Total acceptance doesn't mean that we'd be okay with something if it were just a little more this or that, or after X or Y happens; it means that we take out the judgment that something is wrong or shouldn't be and accept it *exactly as it is, right here, right now, with no conditions.*

If things are really bad or stuck or aren't necessarily as we want them to be, then that last sentence can be pretty challenging to consider. I mean, why would anyone choose to be broke; alone; sick; out of shape; or anything else that feels depressing, frustrating, or painful? We'll resist these things at all costs, because we're afraid that if we don't, we'll get stuck with whatever is causing them. But the truth is that if you are not at peace with your current reality—exactly as it is and exactly as it isn't—then that's exactly when you will get stuck with it. As the famous line goes, "What you resist persists." What you resist you empower. Resistance sucks energy and space, which creates contraction, so when you're spending so much of your precious energy resisting, there is no flow, no life, and definitely no power in that realm.

Coming from *let it be—as it is and as it is not* immediately relieves that contraction, which allows for new insights, attractions, and actions to occur. With this approach, you've given up the resistance and made room for expansion and possibility (here's that idea of creating space for grace again). Whole new worlds open up for you from "just be," as you have the freedom to see the vast landscape from exactly where you're standing.

To put it another way, a student of mine once made a funny but very astute analogy. She said, "You know, what this makes me think of is how I spend all this energy and money buying clothes that will fit me once I lose five pounds. So I have a closet full of nothing to wear. How ridiculous is it that I'm so resistant to being the size that I am that I'll actually spend money on a wardrobe that I wished fit me instead of one that actually does? I mean, I could have so much more fun dressing the body I do have instead of the fantasy one that I think is better!"

We all do this in one way or another. We judge everything from our bodies to our income to our relationships, holding them up to some imaginary ideal that we think is "right," thus making where we are "wrong." The practice of letting it be is about stepping off the treadmill of trying to get somewhere other than where we are.

If what you resist persists, then learn to say *yes!* to every experience, as resisting nothing is the real secret to accessing ease and flow. We begin to dance with new energy in our lives when we remove the judgment that something is wrong here. Just drop that brick of judgment. The naked reality of what you're dealing with will remain—your mother-in-law might still try to control you or you may still be without a job—but you have no judgment about it. It's just what's so. When you take out the thought that something is wrong with your current circumstances, no matter how difficult or painful, it allows you to relax. You can show up fully in your life without feeling as if you need to fix something in order to be at peace. You don't need to be five pounds thinner, wealthier, or more together than you are right now. If you want those things, you can create them, but doing so out of freedom is different from reacting to and resisting what you don't want.

Just to be clear: I'm not talking about settling, condoning, or putting up with anything. There is a huge difference between empowered acceptance and resignation. This isn't about becoming a doormat. Resignation is basically a way of giving up and shutting down, and ultimately a path to powerlessness.

The practice of empowered acceptance leads to a lightness of being. The more you practice this tool, the more you wake up to the total absurdity of resisting life. You begin to access the humor in moments when you catch yourself making things ridiculously hard, needlessly serious, and overly significant. As you gain proficiency with the practice, you can laugh at yourself rather than launching into fault, blame, and shame. You get lighter and playful in the face of difficulty, and you have more fluidity to flow with the bumps on the road and keep your inner peace instead of going to pieces.

"Let It Be" in Action

Here's an exercise you can do that produces powerful results. Think for a moment about a situation in your life that you're not happy with or where the energy is stuck. It can be a relationship, a life circumstance, a health issue—whatever it is that's presenting itself as a complaint in your life and that you wish could be different . . . especially if it's something you're absolutely sure that you can't do much about. The more hopeless it seems, the more likely that it's your golden opportunity!

Now, pick that situation. Fully embrace it, choose it, accept it, and be 100 percent for it *exactly as it is and as it is not.* Literally say out loud, "I embrace _____ exactly as it is, exactly as it isn't." As in:

- "I embrace my mother-in-law exactly as she is, exactly as she isn't."

- "I embrace my son's decision not to go to college exactly as it is, exactly as it isn't."

- "I embrace my bankruptcy exactly as it is, exactly as it isn't."

- "I embrace my relationship with my spouse exactly as it is, exactly as it isn't."

- "I embrace my alcoholism exactly as it is, exactly as it isn't."

- "I embrace my breakup exactly as it is, exactly as it isn't."

- "I embrace my illness exactly as it is, exactly as it isn't."

Notice how right after you say it out loud the voice of doubt in your head says, "Yeah, right . . . sure . . . that was stupid," and so on. As you've been practicing, let those thoughts be and release them.

When we did an exercise similar to this at a workshop in Toronto, a student named Paulina stood up and said that it was her laziness that was presenting the most problems for her. Then she added, "I'm not going to embrace my laziness—no way. I want to overcome it!"

I know we all want to overcome adversity. But remember, we don't *overcome* anything. That's a false sense of control. If Paulina could have worked through her laziness, she would have by now. When we let something be, we're acknowledging it and stepping toward it as a conscious choice. Once we embrace it, we have the freedom to respond to it differently and take a new pathway if that's what we then decide. What we fully choose and embrace we can fully release. There's no power in resisting and being half in or half out. Just be 100 percent for it, as it is and as it isn't without shame, judgment, or complaints, and see what dissolves or arises out of that.

Letting it be is a magic key. It's the space of miracles. Imagine it as though the universe has been trying to get through to you, but because you've got a lot going on in your head and are all bound up with resistance, it's getting a busy signal. But if you relax and let it all be, another line of communication will suddenly be available for you that will allow grace to get through. You don't need to dominate and control things. As you embrace reactivity and resistance, you get to the fear underneath that's driving it in the first place. And when you feel the fear and let that be, too, it dissolves. You just experience it right out of your body.

I have seen this exercise free hundreds of students from the constraints of resistance and resentment. There was Arnold, who chose a difficult situation that had been going on between him and his brother. He shared, "This ongoing conflict with my brother has been the single driving force of my life for the past two years. I'm completely consumed by it. And I see how my resisting the situation has been keeping the dynamic going with the same old anger, righteousness, and fear. So I'm going to embrace it exactly as it is and as it isn't, because now I see that it's also my choice whether to continue to fight or start relating to him in a new way. There's definitely more freedom in that for me."

Then there was Eve, whose three-year-old daughter had Down syndrome. She said, "I choose my daughter's condition. It exists, it's real, and wishing she was different only keeps me from really knowing and loving her."

I also recall Steven, who chose his job situation. "I embrace my layoff," he said. "Up until now, I've just been pissed off about being the victim of something that happened 'to me.' But this is my life—not my boss's or my former company's—and embracing, totally accepting, and choosing what happened and what didn't happen makes it just another chapter of my life story. I am free to create where the story goes from here."

And then there was Travis, who made his fellow workshop participants laugh when he stood up and said, "I choose that my life sucks. No, seriously, I totally embrace it. I get it, and I take full responsibility for it. I'm going to throw myself a 'My life sucks' party and get on with the business of choosing every single part of it that sucks, including my part in creating it! I'm betting that this Grace character Baron talks about will show up to the party and help me out a little in ways I wouldn't expect."

Take on the practice of completely relaxing with what is and letting it all be exactly as it is and as it isn't. Can you give up trying to fix yourself, others, and your circumstances? Whatever you want to change, don't change it. Just let it be. It will let you be. Doing that gives you the freedom to dance with it in a whole new way. Letting it be allows you to discover a new pathway that inspires the heart and is in alignment with what you really want most.

———∽———

CLEAN UP THE MESSES

"Holding on to anger is like grasping a hot coal with the intent of throwing it at someone else: you are the one who gets burned."

— BUDDHA

In "Practice #4: Give it Up to Get Empty," we discussed how we can't create anything new on top of old stuff. That's never been more relevant than when we're talking about the subject of "unfinished business."

You may be holding on to resentments and indignation about how someone wronged you as a way of punishing that other person. Perhaps you think that bitterness is a useful technique of social control; in reality, it does nothing but give you stomach acid and kills off your light. As the Buddha taught, the one you really hurt with your anger and blame is yourself.

There's no way around this: if you want to be of authentic power, you need to clean up and accept the wreckage from your past and in the present.

When we start to wake up to the need for a shift in our life's direction, we can't help but get excited about the possibilities. And that's good—it is exciting. Often we rush forward and make sweeping changes, but the old stuff that held us back previously just keeps coming back and taking over. Until we get really complete with all the unfinished business lurking in the shadows, any sense of personal power we experience is a lie. It's like standing in quicksand: it may look solid, but underneath is actually murky ground.

It always amazes me how much behind-the scenes-conflict goes on within the yoga community. But since it doesn't look good from a yogic perspective, it gets hidden and covered up with flowery philosophy; empty, feel-good language; and fancy technique. At the Baptiste Yoga Centers in Boston and the affiliate centers worldwide, we work to keep honesty, integrity, and open and authentic connections. If we don't, the lines of communication get clogged up with resentments, unsaid feelings, and thoughts that can quickly turn into cynicism and judgments. Then people start isolating themselves, gossiping, acting offensively, or going into whatever survival mode they use to keep themselves in the right.

We have a practice among the teaching staff in our centers that we call "go to your brother" or "go to your sister." Very simply, if we have a problem with anyone, we go directly to that person and get very clear about cleaning stuff up. This is really powerful, because it keeps our energy connected and flowing as a team. Keeping things hidden and talking behind people's backs creates the exact opposite type of power that we're committed to generating for each other and our shared vision. Sure, when feeling hurt or wronged we can always get other people to align with our righteousness and build a little faction, but is that true power?

Imagine going to sleep at night full of knots, knowing that your life is a tangle of pretense, lies, resentments, and secrets. Now picture yourself going from that contraction to living in freedom and authentic connections—with nothing to hide and no unresolved issue constricting your mind. Getting real, coming clean, and telling the truth causes our entire world to shift into a new energetic space of peace and possibility.

The Allure of Being Right

We put so much energy into having to be right. If you think about it, almost all conflict comes out of human beings needing our point of view to be validated as correct. If we weren't so invested in this, we wouldn't get hung up on someone else thinking or behaving in a way that wasn't in line with our position. Resentments arise from our feeling wronged in some way, and most battles we engage in are really just two (or more) people wrestling for control over whose perspective is "the truth."

So what might happen if we simply gave up that need to be right?

I know what you're thinking: *That means you're saying that the other person is right, and you're excusing what he or she said or did.* But I'm not saying that at all. I'm saying there's another way to look at this that might serve you better than the right-wrong game you've been playing up until now.

When you know something *for sure*—as in, you dig your heels in and claim it as a certainty—there's no room for inquiry. There's no possibility to see things about yourself that you might not have seen before or to realize that there are alternate opportunities for creation beyond the story that you already know. But if you're someone who's up to something bigger, and you get that standing

open, undefended, and curious is a chance to keep evolving, then you're aware of the energetic cost and impact
of defending your rightness and how it stops you dead
in your tracks.

This brings to mind a student named Adam, who told
a story about something that had happened to him at
work. One of his co-workers insisted that Adam had gotten an e-mail with certain instructions for a project, but
Adam knew for absolute certain that he never received
it. This turned into a big drama, because his team wasn't
able to complete the project and meet the hard deadline
without that missing piece. Adam stewed about this and
vented to his colleagues and wife for nearly a week, all to
have them agree with him that he was right.

You know how this story ends, don't you? Of course,
Adam had gotten the message—it was sent to his alternate e-mail address. But his insistence didn't allow him to
even *consider* that it had gone to the other account or take
any action with his colleagues other than to complain
and blame. He didn't have the freedom to step back and
contemplate alternative vantage points or plans of action
because all his energy had gone into defending his position and feeling victimized.

Even though this is a really simple example, there
are tons of ways that being right shows up in our lives in
ways big and small. Many of us have been hurt, emotionally and sometimes even physically, and we feel justified
in condemning the character of the person who wronged
us. I'm not suggesting that the awful thing that was done
to us didn't actually happen, nor would I ever minimize
its impact. At the same time, we're here to realize a new
kind of power in ourselves and with others, and those
layers of "It's my fault," "They're to blame," and justified

resentments are standing squarely in our way, keeping us emotionally fragile.

The Cost of Righteousness

Judging other people and situations as wrong in and of itself isn't a bad thing. It is what it is. However, it does come at a price. When we get stuck in a right-versus-wrong paradigm, there's nowhere to go except toward more tension, stress, anxiety, unhappiness, and so on. Typically, when we look closely at the cost, we realize that whatever the payoff to our ego is, the cost outweighs it.

We don't surrender our rightness by giving in and declaring ourselves wrong; that's just another way we'd be right about being wrong. We don't let the other person off the hook or validate what they did (being right is a really juicy morsel to give up, isn't it?). We let go of our rightness simply by our willingness to ask ourselves, "What is being right costing me?" Often the answer to that question is connection, peace of mind, love, real power, our sense of freedom, and our authenticity. We get the satisfaction of feeling right and justified in our position, but really, so what? What does that ultimately do for us?

I saw in my own life how, for a long time, I was operating out of so much righteousness and resentment toward my parents. It was covered up in "Oh, I love them so much," and while that was true, it was a glossing over of this other unspoken issue I had about how they'd wronged me growing up. I eventually had to get myself present to what a self-centered jerk I'd been— I was filled with all this judgment, resentment, and false entitlement—and what that was costing me. Love, connection, intimacy, my energy, my creativity . . . all of these things were being drained from me because I was operating out of "I'm right; they're wrong." When I finally let go of mentally punishing them, gave up the payoff of being the victim, and took complete responsibility for my life, I was freed. My whole life was altered. I came out from hiding and discovered my authenticity; it was a breakthrough into a far brighter, happier existence.

In my experience, rightness is a very powerful brick to give up. To this day, it still rears its head for me. Whenever it does, I can acknowledge its presence and give it up. I keep doing so, again and again, and then create a new way of relating differently out of choice rather than reactivity. From that I can write whatever story I want as the author of my life.

⁓

The need to be right can really limit you. Let's say that someone is giving you feedback, corrections, or coaching advice. What do you do? Most individuals move immediately to defend themselves. If the criticism is heard through your "not good enough" filter, then you take it as negative: "I just can't do anything right," "I blew it," or "I screwed up." Then you probably spin it to make the other guy wrong, explain why you didn't do something as well as you usually do, come up with excuses, or even go on the offensive and attack. If you're angry, you might slam doors. Maybe you stay polite and smile, but inside you're boiling. You internalize it and feel bad about yourself (in which case you still get to be right about how "not enough" you believe you are), get passive-aggressive, or simply believe that the other person is confused and doesn't know what he or she is talking about.

Everyone does this differently. Think about it for a moment: what do you do when you feel attacked? What are the automatic responses that come up?

Fear is behind all of this. When we get feedback, our critical reaction is going to pop up. We feel threatened, so we defend ourselves however we know how. It's pretty simple, actually. Being right is a kind of power born out of fear. We hold on to the rightness, embrace our fear, and take ourselves out. Unfortunately, there's zero power in this behavior.

The reason that this is so important is because you're getting feedback from the world all the time. The question is: How are you holding it? Do you get empowered by it and see it as a chance to grow, or does it take you out? When you're someone who's about being of power and transformation, you start to see how this is a choice. You don't have to accept the feedback as true or right, or reject it as wrong or bad. You can simply hold it as an inquiry in your space and see what comes out of it. Either it will fall away as something you don't feel is useful in your growth, or more people will offer you the same assessment and you will see that maybe there's something to it.

Standing Open and Undefended

The word *ahimsa* is tossed around a lot in the yoga world. It translates loosely to "not doing harm." It's great as a global catchphrase to put on a bumper sticker or a Post-it on the fridge, but it doesn't mean anything until it's put into practice.

Ahimsa begins with the people closest to us. It makes sense, doesn't it? If you want peace on the planet, it needs to start right in your space. For a moment, forget about the White House. What's going on at *your* house? You can scream and yell about wars in the Middle East or Africa, but if you're holding on to resentments and anger, you're doing energetic violence right here—you're contributing to war on the planet by fueling the wars in your own heart and life.

Wars are fought over righteousness. How many people do you know who haven't talked to family members in years because they know they are *right* and the other person is *wrong?* When you hold that kind of anger, you really do need to ask yourself who you're hurting. It's like drinking poison and waiting for the other person to die.

As someone who is of power, you'll want to practice ahimsa right in your own front yard. Embody it by not being willing to engage in the locked-horns game of right and wrong. There is another way, and it's actually astonishingly simple: if you want to win the game, *then just stop playing.* Sidestep it entirely by embodying the way of being you wish to create in your relationship. As Ralph Waldo Emerson said, "What you are comes to you." If you want to create peace, then be of peace. If you want to create compassion, then be of compassion. If you want to create joy, then be of joy.

In the yoga world we call this *taking your seat,* which means getting fully grounded in your space. I've always been so inspired by Gandhi as such a powerful model for this. He didn't "win" his fight by making his oppressors wrong; he simply stood open and undefended for his vision and wasn't engaged in the right-wrong game. He took his seat of self-worth and remained squarely in his intention—his possibility for a new way—and thus transformed the world.

One of my students, a man named Stewart, shared a story with us that I think perfectly exemplifies this practice in everyday life. He and his wife had gone through a painful divorce, and they were both filled with blame and resentment and fought constantly. It was a never-ending battle of wills over who was right about every single thing, from finances to whether their teenage daughter's curfew should be 10:00 or 10:30.

While this was all going on, Stewart came to a bootcamp and had a breakthrough around what his righteousness was costing him and his family, and how futile their struggles were. What was he gaining by fighting to prove his ex-wife wrong all the time? Absolutely nothing. What was lost? A happier life for his daughter and peace of mind for himself.

From that empowered state, Stewart chose to come into the dynamic from a whole other way of being. He gave up his complaints, blame, and need to make his ex-wife wrong. Instead, he started to practice total acceptance of embracing exactly who she is and who she isn't and not getting stuck on any position. He stayed malleable, responding to her in the spirit of the collaborative relationship he wanted to create with her. He treated her with respect and appreciation, and even tried to help her out now and then. If she launched into one their familiar arguments that would typically trigger him, he would successfully practice being open and calm and respond with the suggestion of a compromise that was in the best interest of their child. Stewart did this again and again—as many times as it took to make it real. He was a pitbull for a positive, new vision. Eventually, she got on board with the shift, and a collective, harmonious relationship emerged as a result of his giving up his rightness. He was now able to relate to his ex-wife from a new, creative freedom rather than the resistance-filled realm of "make her wrong."

It's always our choice to be of power, regardless of whether someone else shares that mind-set at the time or not. It's never about what another person does or says; it's about keeping your eyes on the prize of a new possibility for yourself, others, and the connection that can bring about transformation.

You want to start calling yourself out every time you notice fault and blame come up. It's a brick that you can bring into view, as in, "Oh, yeah, there it is again." Each time you see it, give it up. Again and again, let it go . . . on the other side is the opportunity to take full responsibility for your choices in how you react.

The question is never who is right; you automatically lose the minute you start that game. The true question is, "What is being right costing me?" and then, "What am I up to in my life, and how can I stand in a new way of being that fulfills me?"

Like Gandhi, be what you want to see. Stand firmly in whatever new way of being you are looking to create in your relationships, and very quickly you'll see your reality line up with your intentions in every way.

Releasing Resentments

It can be difficult to rise above the right-wrong game if you feel betrayed, the way Michael did. He owned two thriving Baptiste affiliate studios in Texas, when one of his head teachers left and opened her own studio only a few blocks away, taking a big chunk of his community (and business) with her. Needless to say, this was a huge blow. Here's how Michael described it:

"I was infuriated! I responded by insisting that my studio manager ask this teacher not to practice at our studios anymore. I went into a blame and anger spiral. I became very caught up in being right and making her wrong. I even told folks how I saw this coming and that she was never really on our team. After all, I was her teacher. I trained her. Is this what I get after giving her so much? I felt betrayed."

The resentment festered for a long time, until Michael came to ask me for some coaching on how to relieve the situation. I told him that I knew him to be a powerful teacher and a leader in his community, and that he wasn't coming from that authentic space when relating to his former employee. I gently asked him, "What do you need to give up?" and suggested that he already knew what he had to do: drop the brick of judgment and clean up the mess between them. I explained that without getting complete in this issue, his valuable energy would always be tangled up in it.

So Michael went to this woman and asked if they could talk. Here's how the rest of the story goes, directly from him:

> I asked for her forgiveness for being judgmental and righteous, and for gossiping about her. I explained that this is not who I am. I told her that I'm a leader in the yoga community (as well as her teacher), and I wanted to work with her in building our community to greatness, not

destroying it. My thoughts, feelings, and actions of being right were destroying the possibility of creating anything abundant—for her and for me. She asked for my forgiveness as well. I felt so free and full of love after our conversation. I felt a big weight lift, as if this huge vacuum of negativity and anger in my body disappeared, and joy and light came streaming in.

A few weeks later, I attended her yoga studio's grand opening. It was one of the most challenging things I'd done in my life as I walked solo toward the entrance of her new studio. A lot of people stared at me, wondering why I was there. It was in that moment I realized that this is what it means to be a leader in my community beyond my studio walls—to show up with courage and strength for others, not just for myself. In that moment, something that Baron always says struck me: "You are either an example or a warning." I want to be an example.

A question for when any of us needs to transform a judgment or negative thought into a more empowered view is, "What do I need to take my attention *off* of, and what do I need to put my attention *on?*" Michael freed himself from the right-wrong game that was killing his energy by shifting his vision toward the bigger picture of what he is up to in his life, which is being a leader who empowers others in his community.

The "How" of Forgiveness

Often people don't understand what's involved in the act of forgiving. It's common to believe that if we absolve someone who did something wrong, hurt us, or deceived us, it's as if we're saying that we're okay with what he or she did . . . but just that once. The unsaid condition is, "But they'd better not do it again!" This kind of forgiveness doesn't free us from the past, because we're still holding on to fault and blame. We may in fact have been victimized, hurt, and harmed—and we absolutely don't want to condone that—but if we keep blame alive inside us, we revictimize ourselves internally and energetically, over and over. And, as we know, that comes at a cost.

There's a story of two vets from the Korean War who were in a prison camp together where they were tortured. They met at a dinner many years later, not having seen each other since the war. One of the men asked the other, "Have you forgiven our captors?"

The other answered, "Absolutely not. I will never forgive them for what they did to me."

The first one replied, "Well, then you're still in that prison."

It's kind of like that. Even though stuff may have happened to us a long time ago, something has to shift inside, and we need to fully let it go. Otherwise, we're still held captive to it. True forgiveness involves making space inside ourselves that enables us to rise above the past and leave it behind.

While of course the circumstances of that last story were very real, what's interesting is that a lot of resentments are unfounded and ungrounded in reality. When you get present and really look at what happened, you may notice that the person you're upset with didn't actually do what you thought he or she did. Your belief might be an interpretation you created in your own mind—a story you made up about it. Maybe it reminded you of something from your past, you felt scared, or you were threatened. In Michael's case, for example, his former employee may not have set out to take away his students and be divisive within their community. It's very possible that she was just looking to spread her wings as a teacher, leader, and entrepreneur and happened to have the financial circumstances to make that happen. It's also possible that she didn't act in total integrity while all this was happening.

What I'm getting to here is that we may be convinced that our viewpoint is right—that it's the *truth*—but there may be more to consider than what we're seeing (remember Adam, who was certain he did not receive that wayward e-mail?).

I do an exercise with my students that can help you open up your thinking about this. I call this the Voice of God exercise, because it shows us how we hold our point of view as the absolute truth when, in fact, there might be more to consider:

> — Choose one person in your life whom you have some kind of conflict or unsettled energy with. It can be anyone. (I'm guessing you probably didn't have to think too hard to come up with someone.)

> — Take out a piece of paper and write everything that isn't okay about this individual. What's wrong with him? Where is she incorrect

in her thinking? How has he wronged you? Refrain from using any enlightened viewpoints or spiritual spiels, and instead just write as if you were letting it rip to someone you're really close to. Just shoot straight about what you think the person needs to change about him/herself.

— Next, write your justifications for keeping your point of view alive about this person. You must have good reasons for not giving it up, so get them all down.

— Now write, *I don't know the whole truth about this person.* Then just see what comes out of that. We live as though we know the whole truth, but consider that it's possible that you can't honestly and accurately describe anything or anyone, because it's always subjective. All you have is a description—just a story about something that happened in the past or is going on in the present.

If you come from "I don't know the truth about this person," as in you really acknowledge that you don't know the whole truth, then what might be possible with that individual? What kind of healing, clearing, and new opportunities could be available?

A last word here about the practice of forgiveness: you want to give up the assumption that just because you're doing your part in forgiving, your friend, co-worker, or family member should, too. It's nice when that happens, sure, but sometimes the person may need to just sit with it or see you demonstrate your new way of being for a while. This is an act of generosity that you're ultimately doing for yourself, so you can have a more authentic life. If any part of this is a strategy to get someone to apologize to you or accept blame, please know that typically doesn't turn out so well.

Nothing anyone does can ever earn our mercy; nothing someone says or does can make up for whatever it is we're holding against them. Pure and simple, as with anything we give with an open heart, the gifts of forgiveness will come back to us tenfold.

Accepting the Unacceptable

It's especially difficult to give up being right when we see loved ones harming themselves the way Andrea did. She shared, "I love my mom . . . I admire her and am inspired by her. But she works way too hard and has been doing so for 40 years. She's starting to have health issues that I don't think she's acknowledging. Her body is falling apart, and she just won't do anything about it. I keep telling her, 'Oh, you should live a more balanced life,' and we have this ongoing tension because she's more committed to her work than her health. It's a huge battle between us. I know I'm right, because taking care of herself is important, and I'm not going to let go of being right here, because her well-being is at stake."

I think pretty much everyone can relate to this in one way or another. Maybe you know of certain individuals who are harming themselves, who would be better off if they would just listen to you . . . and maybe you're right.

But what you want to look at is the energy that's coming up here; it's all about resistance, control, winning, or losing. You're locking horns, and in turn creating a dead end. It's beautiful that Andrea is so concerned about her mother's health. At the same time, her approach in coming from rightness isn't getting her the results she wants or empowering her mom. Unfortunately, they're both left feeling diminished.

I suggested to Andrea that she give up her expectation of what her mother should be doing and stop making her wrong. We all want peace, and the way we get it is by taking out the idea that something is wrong here—that something needs to be fixed. What if Andrea just accepted her mother exactly as she is and as she isn't and approached the relationship with only love and total acceptance? And then, from that softened perspective of acceptance, Andrea might start to see new opportunities to empower her mom.

When you give up the hard stance that you're sure you're right, suddenly a panoramic view opens up. It's like seeing 360 degrees instead of just through a telescope.

Andrea tried this and noticed a difference almost immediately. By taking her seat in her intention of loving and accepting her mother, she saw how she could take care of herself more visibly when she was around her mom—and by putting out that energy, inspire her mom to do the same. She stopped yelling at her mother that she should go to the gym, and instead they got together two mornings each week to go for a long walk.

When you come from a place of inspiration and sharing rather than judgment and control, people won't feel invalidated or the need to defend and resist and will in turn be more likely to be open to hearing what you're saying. With this one small brick removed, you can radically transform the energy in your relationships.

Taking Responsibility for Ourselves . . . and Our Lives

At some point in my 20s, I woke up and realized that my life was messed up. I was lost and confused, and I had all this pain and anxiety I was dragging around with me. I went through a lot of self-examination and eventually came to what I thought was *the truth* about how I'd become this way: it was because of my childhood, how my parents had neglected me, and so on. I felt very sure that clearing the air between us was critical, so I went home to San Francisco bearing the truth as if it were some kind of torch that was going to light up our relationship. I went to forgive my parents for all the ways they had screwed me up.

It did not go well.

Needless to say, my mom and dad didn't feel that they had done anything wrong, so my arriving on their doorstep with a grand proclamation about how I was forgiving them for all their transgressions didn't fall on welcome ears. They felt that they'd always done their best, and suddenly I was appearing telling them how awful they had been . . . *but that I forgave them.* At the time, I couldn't see why this didn't work or make me feel any better.

Essentially, my parents and I didn't talk for two years after that. I went away and did more work on myself, expanding my understanding of what had gone wrong there, and eventually I realized, *Oh, I didn't take responsibility.* I was taking responsibility for my anger, but still putting the blame on them for causing it in the first place. The clearing that needed to happen here was not in my forgiving them, but in their releasing me for having held them in such judgment for all these years.

I went back a second time, two years later, and simply thanked them for giving me life. In a genuine way, I gave them credit for everything good that I have. I've received so many great things from my parents, but prior to showing them my gratitude, I couldn't recognize or appreciate any of it. All I could see is what they'd done wrong, all the stuff I didn't like, and the things I rejected. For years I blamed *them* for what wasn't working in *my* life.

Going back a second time, I took ownership and said, "Everything that's great in my life, you gave me. Thank you. Everything else, that's me—I'm an adult now, and I'm responsible. And I just want to say I'm sorry, because I held an emotional sword over you and I judged you."

It was such an opening, since I wasn't giving them anything to resist or fight against. What came out of that day was pretty amazing. There was acceptance present in our relationship, which had never happened before, and from there I really got to know my mom for the first time. She opened up to me about her own childhood, and I gained a whole new perspective on what an amazing woman she is and the life she's lived—a true sense of who she was.

My dad also opened up in his own way. He'd always been pretty closed off emotionally toward me, and I resented this until I found out why. He'd grown up during the Great Depression as the eldest of 11 kids, and when he was 13 his mom abandoned them for another man. His father worked three jobs just to sustain them, so my dad became the caretaker of all his siblings. He never really had a parent. In the Depression, Oprah wasn't around yet to tell us how to do it right as parents. I suddenly realized, *Whoa . . . he really comes from a different world than I grew up in.* I started having real, true compassion for my dad. I could see how in his own way, even though he was emotionally bound up, he'd always shown up with his own expression of love and care for our family.

Becoming aware of this blind spot was a breakthrough for me. I was finally able to *see* my parents, not just my idea about them. It took getting to total forgiveness and acceptance to digest the uncommon insight and incredible life lessons passed down to me by my father, a legendary yoga master whose message profoundly transcended the world of physical yoga. The practice of meditation, which was at the very core of his message, has increasingly become a source of tremendous power in my own life and the many transformed lives of the people he touched. The more I wake up as a student of yoga and transformation, the more I recognize how unquestionably my father is still a man way ahead of his time.

By taking responsibility for judging him, I actually healed something deep inside. Where prior to this fundamental shift I could only notice the shadow side of my father in me, I can now recognize all of his extraordinary qualities within me. He left his body in August 2001, and I am deeply and forever touched by his guidance and spiritual teaching and deeply appreciative that he always pointed me in the direction of personal development and learning more about myself.

Cleaning up the disempowering stories I had about my parents allowed me to finally put to rest events in my life that I had tried in vain to bury. When I healed my relationship with my dad, I found my own sense of masculinity. I also gained a deeper understanding into the importance of a father in a child's life, which was a breakthrough for me in parenting my own kids. Connecting with my mom allowed me to heal my relationship with all women—including my ex-wife—and create connections with them that are unconstrained by the past. My being stuck in many different areas of my life immediately disappeared as I let go of the blame, resentment, and the need to be right. On the other side was a new kind of power and freedom waiting for me.

ᔟ

Taking responsibility starts with healing the fractures in our closest relationships, which are often the most challenging. You've heard the saying, "You only hurt the ones you love," and deep down you probably know that's true. It takes courage to come clean, tell the truth, and call yourself out in the context of these relationships, usually because resentments have had a lifetime to build and gain steam in our minds. Healing these fractures heals the fractures in our own hearts.

Taking responsibility also requires humility—the willingness to see how we've acted and recognize that it's not who we want to be. It's never too late. As the Turkish proverb goes, "No matter how far down a wrong road you go, turn back." Ideally, as we become wiser, maybe we go down the wrong road but we don't go quite as far. We correct our course sooner and restore our authenticity. We have those difficult, heart-to-heart conversations; start being real; and own what we're responsible for—not tomorrow . . . not next week . . . but today. Right now. This is it. All we've really got is right now.

I'll end this chapter with a story about a course participant named Alan, who was a very accomplished and wealthy guy. Through a lot of his climbing the success ladder, Alan had been kind of a bully and a jerk and created a lot of emotional wreckage for the people around him. When he came to one of our trainings, he really took on the practice of cleaning up those messes; he went home and owned up to how he'd behaved to the people in his life. He apologized and asked to be forgiven for the impact his actions had on his friends, co-workers, and family members. He listened, acknowledged other people's perceptions and feelings about what had gone on in the past, and let them know how he appreciated them for who they had been for him.

About a month later, Alan passed away unexpectedly. I know this because his wife called to thank me. She said he died with a feeling of completion and peace of mind because he had made good with the people in his life. I'd always known this practice was powerful stuff, but when I heard this, even I thought, *Wow.*

Life is amazing that way. Alan had some type of spiritual urgency to clean up his messes without even knowing why, and he immediately went and acknowledged all that he needed to. I'm not saying that our lives need to be threatened in order to have this practice be powerful for us; exactly the opposite. What I *am* saying is, why wait? We can live powerfully by doing it right here, right now.

———⌒———

EMBRACE NAKED REALITY

"Among the great things which are found among us, the existence of Nothing is the greatest."

— LEONARDO DA VINCI

Things happen in our daily lives that are good, bad, or otherwise. Every day, we have interactions with people and experiences ranging from the exciting to the mundane. In and of themselves, these events have no charge. Our challenges arise when we give them meaning. We create all kinds of stories around the stuff that happens—what it means about us, others, our relationships, our status, and so on. Those stories weigh us down, create stress and discomfort, and—if we pile them on for years and years—disease.

Here's an example from Scarlett, the mother of two-year-old twins. The night before she was leaving to come to a workshop with me, her toddlers—whom she described as being in their "terrible twos"—got into some mischief and decided to smear an entire tub of ointment in their hair. Scarlett was in the process of packing and getting ready to leave town for a week, so she was quite aggravated that she had to drop everything to help her children clean up a sticky mess. She finally got them cleaned off and went upstairs to pack. When she returned not even five minutes later, they'd made another huge mess by painting on the floor. That was it. Mom lost it and started screaming at them.

Things like this happen all the time (especially when we're dealing with kids!). The problem wasn't that Scarlett's twins made a mess. It was that she *made the experience mean something.* She interpreted the actions of her two-year-olds as proof that, as she put it, "I never get to do anything for myself . . . I'm trapped . . . they're out to get me . . . my life is out of control. . . ."

An empowering question in any challenging situation would be: *Can you see the difference between what actually happened—the naked reality—and the drama you created around it that's giving it weight and charge? Even more, are you willing to drop those stories, knowing that layering on all that meaning and interpretation is blocking your natural power and flow?* Such questions speak to what you're committed to: your stories versus your transformation to being of power. We choose the latter when we quickly get to the facts of what's happening in a situation rather than being stuck in the opinions and explanations we're adding to what's going on.

What *actually happened* is what you want to get to here. So really, what happened? In Scarlett's case, her children put ointment in their hair. Okay, that happened. That's the naked reality. They were full-on having a party, smearing it on their heads and doing whatever kids do. Their mom, though, interpreted the facts as something catastrophic. But there are lots of other ways she could have approached the situation, right? Maybe the twins wanted to imitate their mom putting styling products in her hair and were modeling her beauty routine. Or what if they were just being creative and expressive or simply having fun? The power here lies in seeing that you have the freedom to choose how you view events, and, as a result, how you respond. When you come from a neutral, relaxed place, you create the space to handle the situation in a nonreactive way (as I talked about in "Practice #5: Let It Be") as you see appropriate.

Embracing naked reality is a practice of seeing the difference between what actually is and the garbage we add to it. Our work here is to step back, take a clear look at the bare facts, and distinguish them from our own fiction. Here's the beauty of it: that which we create, we can undo and then create anew.

Our Point of View

We live our entire existence out of our own point of view. Actually, we don't even have a point of view. We *are* a point of view. That's how confident each of us is in our belief that we're seeing the truth. We wear different lenses through which we perceive our world, never taking into consideration that they determine *what* we see. They funnel our attention to only certain aspects of reality or a situation. We don't see the world in front of us, and we don't see the filter; rather, we only see what the filter allows us to see.

There is a retreat center I go to in Hawaii where they wrap the main hall—which is a big, pavilion-type building in the jungle—in heavy sheets of plastic so we can keep the heat inside when we do our physical practice (Baptiste Yoga is done in a warm room). It makes for an interesting experience, because the participants, staff, and I are basically enclosed in a plastic bubble for a week during these sessions. Many students have a lot of feelings and interpretations about the so-called bubble, so one time I asked everyone to list them. Here's just a small sample of what we got:

The bubble is . . .

+ . . . stuffy.

+ . . . enveloping.

+ . . . annoying.

+ . . . ridiculous.

+ . . . an incubator of transformation.

+ . . . a greenhouse for growth.

+ . . . a warm refuge.

+ . . . constricting.

The naked reality is that the bubble is none of those things. Those are just interpretations that the participants gave it, as seen through their own lens. If people are coming from a place of feeling constricted, they'll see this space as limiting and stuffy. If they're annoyed, they'll see the bubble as irritating and ridiculous. If they're weary or were cold that morning, they'll see it as a warm refuge. But really, the bubble simply is what it is. It's a large-sized room, with two doorways, wrapped in clear plastic sheeting—nothing more, nothing less.

Here's another way to think about point of view. Students often point to their heads and say that they feel stuck "in here." But there isn't actually any reality to that. Life happens outside of us. The filters we have about what's out there are in fact all in our heads coloring our perception. In other words, as the philosopher Goethe said, "You don't see life as it is. You see life as you are." We want to take off the filters to get back to what's called *samadhi,* meaning "neutral vision." In Sanskrit, *sama* means "neutral" or "clear," and *dhi* is "vision." It's not colored, there is nothing added to block or limit our clear view.

Have you ever come out of an amazing yoga class or a deeply relaxing meditation with an expanded awareness beyond yourself, yet you were still fully grounded in your body and senses? It's as if you suddenly saw and heard everything more vividly and felt more alive and aware. For example, maybe you had a conversation with a friend and could *really* hear this person. That happens because you've removed the filters and are fully experiencing life in its purest expression.

When we're trapped in our own point of view, the energy gets depressed and repressed. The stories, interpretations, and meanings we give to experiences are the filters we need to drop in order to come to the empowering state of samadhi.

Drop Your Stories

Not long before coming to a bootcamp in Costa Rica, Christina had radically changed her life when she left her longtime job—which, she admitted, had been her whole identity up until then. She was ready for something new, but didn't really have a plan for what was up next. She said she was excited, though, because she was going to do some traveling through New Hampshire in the meantime. Yet then she immediately followed that up with, "Even though that seems really scary."

We broke it down: what was scary? Was she afraid she wasn't going to have a place to sleep? No. That she wouldn't have enough money to eat? No. Encounter bodily harm? No. Was she afraid of the people she was going to meet? No. "Scary" was just what Christina unconsciously made up about her upcoming trip.

The mind gives meaning to everything that happens in the past or that we believe will take place in the future, and that becomes our story. And we love our stories, because they tell us who we are. A deep purification and transformation occurs when we have a breakthrough in seeing that *nothing has any meaning except the one we give it.*

The practice of embracing naked reality is very simple. When you find yourself spinning a story about anything—and you'll know you're spinning a story if you feel yourself becoming worked up, stressed out, or fearful—pause, get present to your body, breathe, and simply ask yourself, "What's actually going on here?" At its bare-naked, raw form, what's happening? What are the plain facts?

For instance: "My boss was unhappy with my work on a project and requested that I redo it," "My husband was late for our dinner reservation," or "I forgot to send my tax form in." When you come at the situation from that facts-only perspective, you'll start to experience space around it and land fully in the present moment. You can just be with the experience as it is and actively choose how to relate to it . . . and then calmly plot out your course of action from there. You can choose to revise the project, ask your husband if the traffic was bad, or call your accountant and set the necessary paperwork in motion rather than automatically launching into fantasy stories of, "I'm going to get fired," "My husband never respects my time or feelings," and "I'm a screwup who will end up in the poorhouse." That freedom of choice is a tremendous source of power.

We don't know what options are available to us if we don't create that space between ourselves and our automatic response. Dropping all the meaning, Scarlett could just be with her two-year-olds as they are, without the filter of "They're in their terrible twos" or "This is a catastrophe." Yes, there was still a mess to clean up, and she still might have felt aggravated, but she could have also laughed at the absurdity of the situation, which would have a totally different impact than raging and screaming.

૭

You know how you sometimes get all choked up when you tell a story about an event in your life? Well, that's a clear signal that you're carrying around an interpretation of the experience that's weighing you down. The story creates emotion, and as a result you feel controlled and constrained. You're not free from it. Tales from the past are the ones that most inhibit us; we keep the experiences and feelings alive in our minds and bodies, as though they're still happening. The past isn't anything but a memory, yet we're still holding on to an old story as if it's occurring right now.

On the other hand, take a moment right now and think of a situation that you've completely let go of. It can be an event from the distant past or even something that you've recently moved beyond. How do you feel when you imagine talking about it? Clean and clear, right? That's what I mean by being free. The triumph from releasing the story creates the opening to ask a key question, which is, "What's possible from here?"

The heavy meaning you add on top of your experiences is the root of all stress. Everyone does it; no one is alone in this practice. Life happens, and you automatically veer into story land. Your spouse forgets to pick up the dry cleaning: it means she doesn't value all you do for her. Your boyfriend doesn't call you back: it means that he's pulling away from you. Your kids create a huge mess: it means that you're trapped in a life of chaos and no one respects you. You lose your job: it means you're doomed, maybe even pathetic—or worse, a total failure.

Consider that you live in a world full of inflated significance, and that's why you're so exhausted. Pour on all that meaning, and you'll feel energetically heavy. Let go of it, though, and you're in the domain of freedom, energy, and power. The following saying comes from the first Noble Truth of the Buddha: "Pain is inevitable, but suffering is optional." Perhaps there is real pain from an experience, but your suffering can be greatly lessened by letting go of the junk you've piled on top of it. Having no story allows you the space to create a new, empowering one. And when we live from that, life is a creative act.

Dealing with Emotional Upset

A student named Marco once shared this at a retreat I was leading in Montana:

"This morning I hiked about a mile up to where I could get cell reception in order to call home. I had all this incredible stuff I wanted to tell my wife about my week here, but she was distracted and totally focused on dealing with the plumber coming to fix a pipe that was leaking. I hung up the phone feeling very hurt, like she didn't care at all about what I was saying or what I was experiencing."

We all get wounded like this, sometimes daily. We take what someone else does or says personally, which takes us immediately out of our power. Or we feel disappointed, offended, insulted, not wanted, and so on, and this leads to distress. Over time, it can start to become death by a thousand tiny cuts, as these emotional upsets drain our energy and life force.

It can be pretty automatic to make someone wrong the moment you realize that your expectations aren't being met. Unknowingly at that moment, you're usually triggered by some situation from your past. You leave the present entirely, and anyone speaking to you becomes a character from a previous time or event. Into every situation you naturally bring your point of view and old stories, which are things you believe to be true about yourself, such as, "No one cares about me." Or maybe it's an old, familiar complaint you have running in the background of your life, as in, "My wife never listens to me." Communication with the actual person who's there in that present circumstance gets weird, because you're not really relating to the individual as he or she is, as things are, in unfiltered reality.

It's typical in an upsetting situation like this to pretend that you're not upset and that you're not making someone or something wrong, even though you are. When you do this, you become inauthentic, and others experience you as being off. The question you want to get to here, once again, is, "What is it costing me to hold on to this resentment or upset?" That's the immediate path that allows you to give it up, because you can see the peace of mind that it's robbing you of.

It's a helpful practice to get specific regarding what you're upset about. Get very clear: *He or she did or said what, exactly, and what did I interpret that to mean?* That instantly brings you right back to the naked reality of the moment. When you get present and really look, you might notice that the individual didn't actually do whatever it is you're upset about. A lot of resentments are ungrounded in reality, simply misfirings of the mind. Or maybe they actually did or said the thing that angered you, in which case you have the opportunity to give up the brick of resentment and quickly get back to what you were up to before.

All that happened when Marco called home was that his wife was focused on getting a plumber to come to the house. That is the naked reality. Marco, however, made it mean that he wasn't important to her . . . that his experiences weren't of interest to her . . . maybe even that she didn't love him enough. He created all of it, probably because it reminded him of something from his past (or a dynamic from their shared past as a couple). He felt scared and threatened because he had "evidence" from their interaction ("she was distracted") that proved him right.

In my own thinking, I always want to get to whether or not it's useful for me to be stuck on whatever emotional upset is derailing me. Is it allowing me to be a yes in my continual evolution and to what I'm committed to in my heart? Or is it a brick that I need to drop so that I can free myself and be of power? Since it's a story I created in my own mind, it's all mine, and so I'm the one who has complete and total say in the matter. I'm also the one who pays the piper with my energy. If it's not serving me, others, or the planet, then I let it go, because I'm up to something bigger than that. I take ownership of my own experiences and feelings and interact with people in regard to what's going on right now, not the things they did back in the past, or even some random event from long ago that just got triggered.

Whenever you find yourself tangled in an emotional upset, remember to pause, get grounded in your body, breathe, and distinguish between what's actually going on in your environment and what's going on in your head. Like we said earlier in "Practice #6: Clean Up the Messes," notice what you need to take your focus *off* and what you need to put it back *on*. It's a small but powerful shift in perception.

Embodied Fear

I once saw a large iguana in Mexico stop, as if frozen, when a cloud came between it and the sun. It wasn't going to risk being wrong about the shadow, which could have been a hawk in the sky looking for a snack. It made me wonder: considering how we tend to live by automatic response, how often do we get paralyzed by perceived threats?

Everything we see, hear, smell, touch, and taste gets sent directly to what's been called the *reptilian brain:* a small, primitive area of the brain that instinctively determines if a signal we've received poses a threat to our survival. If so, it reacts. The problem is that the whole process flies underneath the radar of our normal awareness, so fear can end up running our lives more often than we know. The even bigger issue is this: we don't know that we don't know. The reptilian brain is okay with not being accurate and erring on the side of keeping us safe. Even if the threat of danger is false, an alarm gets raised, and we react to anything that even remotely resembles a past threat.

Here's how this plays out in our everyday lives. Something happens, and our nervous system goes automatically into fight, flight, or freeze. We recognize the body signals that let us know we're in danger—pounding heart, sweaty palms, throat locking up, arms heavy—and we react. That's the fear that becomes present whenever our reptilian brains perceive a threat. Of course, if we were confronted by a snarling grizzly bear in the wild, or if a stranger approached us on the street in an aggressive way, our automatic survival response would be a good thing, because it would serve to protect us. But that's not the case when it kicks in during day-to-day situations, as in minor conflicts and confrontations. Or worse, it reacts to a random threatening thought in our head and our body experiences it as real.

What you want to notice is how you're relating to fear when it shows up. Is it automatically taking you out, or can you see that it's a reaction that's probably out of alignment with the actual level of threat? A bear? Yeah, that's scary. That's a reason to freeze and play dead. Speaking to other human beings? Not so scary in reality.

Yet since our "fear body" doesn't know the difference, it automatically kicks in. We tend to think that if we're physically having this reaction, we must be in danger—that's how real it feels. The emotions and body chemistry are real, but is the story? Or is it an interpretation all made up in the mind?

Everyone has his or her own typical adaptation response to fear. Maybe you get light-headed, your heart pounds, you have difficulty focusing, or you get a headache or stomachache. It's really powerful to identify yours, because when those body sensations show up, they're a signal to pause and ask that pivotal question of, "What's actually happening?"

At a workshop in upstate New York, a participant named Jacqueline received a message from the front desk that her father had called. Hearing from her dad wasn't a usual thing, especially when she was away on retreat with no cell-phone service. Immediately, Jacqueline felt her whole body go tense and break out in a cold sweat— her typical fear adaptation response. Her physical self signaled that there was a looming threat, so her mind was further charged up. She suddenly imagined tragedies of all kinds that must have gone on at home. Near hysteria, she got to the front desk only to find a message that said, "Your mom and I decided to go out of town for a few days, so we'll be out of reach in case you try to call."

That was it. No tragedy. But no one told Jacqueline's parasympathetic nervous system that. Her body sensations were signaling *Danger! Danger!* so she instantaneously went into reactive survival mode. That's how fast it happens.

This is valuable information, because when you feel your fear show up, you can take it as a signal to pause, get present in your body, find the source of the fear, and really look at it with clear eyes. You can look at the naked reality of the situation—just the raw facts—and ask, "What's actually happening? What's the actual threat? Is this really so scary? What's scary about it?" You'll likely notice that *scary* usually lives in your mind.

Fear happens when you get all caught up in your thoughts—you isolate from what's really going on out there and start spinning stories. Maybe some things are frightening, but most of the time they're nowhere near as bad as all the stuff you've made up about them. Just like Christina's story about traveling that I shared earlier—she was going to New Hampshire, for goodness' sake! I haven't been there in a long time, but my recollection is that the people there aren't all that terrifying.

The key to making fear disappear is to root ourselves down in reality. Remember that what we actually, physically see is the present reality. We're either in story land or right here. Wherever our feet are on Earth is our path of power. For the most part, everything else is our reptilian brain in survival mode, creating meaning and spinning stories.

In my upper-level trainings, I work with people from all walks of life on how to be authentic and effective with and in front of groups. You probably already know that public speaking tops the list of common fears, so it makes sense that most individuals initially experience a walk through the fire of fear. But none of their fear-based adaptation responses help them to be more powerful or free in their sharing with others. I've never heard a student say, "If only my heart raced, my mind went blank, my mouth went dry, and I disconnected from my audience in front of me . . . *then* I could experience total connection and give an amazing presentation."

You don't have to be a yoga teacher or public speaker in order to recognize what I'm saying here. It's common to feel fear if you're speaking about something that's important to you, or if you're taking a stand or confronting someone about a difficult issue. You may have even become good at isolating yourself to prevent this from happening.

Power; peace of mind; and the freedom of communicating powerfully all the time, everywhere, and with everyone all come from the practice of flowing from your grounded center rather than from fear. That's why it's so important that you are in a practice of fully experiencing it, dancing with it, and acting in the face of it, rather than reacting to the auto response that's hardwired into your nervous system.

This mechanistic survival system can keep us living inside a virtual box that protects us from anything unknown, new, and unpredictable. Unfortunately, that includes being closed off from wonderful opportunities that are only found through defying the predictable, disrupting business as usual and expanding into uncharted horizons.

———ℒ———

PRACTICE #8

DEFY THE LIE

"[E]ven the truth, when believed, is a lie."

— WERNER ERHARD

Of all the tools in this book, this one is the heart. All that you've been doing so far has led you here—to a fundamental practice that can cause a seismic shift in your entire way of being. Perhaps this sounds dramatic, but that's how powerful it is when you root out the lie that's been ruling your life and declare, "No more."

In "Practice #7: Embrace Naked Reality," we explored how we suffer not because difficult things happen, but because of the meaning we give to those events. And this is never more impactful than when we let pivotal events in our lives make us believe that something is true about *who we are.*

Here's how it works. It begins with something painful or challenging that happened in our past. It could have been a difficult incident or an experience of loss, big or small, that we perhaps consider significant. Whatever it was had an effect on us, because we took it personally. We made it mean something about ourselves, as in we're not good enough, smart enough, pretty enough, skinny enough, worthy enough, desirable enough, loveable enough, and so on. We internalize that lie and transmute it into the truth in our minds; thus, it becomes a deep belief system.

Although totally unconscious to it, that's the perspective from which we go about our lives.

For instance, here is April's story:

"When I was 12, something relatively small happened that I now see has shaped everything I've done my entire life. I used to do ballet, which I didn't like but my parents made me commit to. My real love was soccer—that's what I was passionate about. They let me play on a team, but ballet was their big focus for some reason.

One afternoon, my mom was late picking me up from ballet to get to my soccer match. She was nowhere to be found. I called her at work, but she wasn't there. I ended up missing the tournament, and it was the biggest deal to me. Now it doesn't seem like much, but at the time I thought, *My mom doesn't care about me. I'm not a priority. She forgot about me.* And then I got this thought loud and clear: *I am alone . . . I have to take care of myself.*"

Let's say that you feel alone like April—as in, deep down in your bones you believe that you're isolated in the world and the only person you can really rely on is yourself. So as a way to cope, you become extremely independent. You make being on your own okay. Maybe you're even proud of how self-reliant you are, and that's definitely an accomplishment. Still, underneath you're left with that inner lonely world. You're trying to fix something that can't be fixed on the outside, because it's a lie to begin with. Well, you're not alone if you look at the naked reality here. That's just a belief you made up, decided was true when you were younger, and have chosen, albeit unconsciously, to buy into ever since.

This wasn't a traumatic event, per se, but it had an impact on April's mind. It became self-defining, and thus shaped how life has shown up for her. There are many among us who have experienced the same result. Take Trescott, for example, who, at the age of eight, watched as his mother was attacked in their home by an intruder. I wouldn't dare to minimize the impact of something such as that. What I'm focusing on, though, is what he then made it mean: that he wasn't safe. His entire adult life revolved around being betrayed, abandoned, or hurt by friends, lovers, and co-workers—even by the tent mate he'd just met at his Baptiste Yoga Teacher Training in upstate New York, who he was certain had stolen his expensive yoga mat (it ended up that Trescott had left it behind in the yoga room).

I've heard many people tell highly charged stories of past events: for example, childhood abuse, rape, or bankruptcy. And to each one of them, along with my sincere compassion, I offer this insight: the story, as it is, doesn't exist anymore. What happened absolutely happened—it's real. But it means nothing now, because it's gone. It took place in the past, which no longer exists; only the description of it and the meaning that's been assigned to it still do.

All we have is right here, right now. Something that already occurred is only a story. Even if it affected our physical being, the body eventually becomes neutral; after all, our cells turn over and the body completely reinvents itself every seven years or so. But the mind runs its narrative, and that's what keeps the experience energetically alive. The significance we placed upon an event in the past keeps it significant in the present. We lose our real power to the story—but here, once and for all, we can get it back.

At some point you've probably made a declaration similar to this: "I'm all alone. I'm not safe. I'm a freak.

I'm not worthy of love. I'm stupid." You gave yourself a judgment and have been living with it as a silent belief of "that's just who I am." But it's not actually who you are; it's just something you made up. When you really get this insight, it changes everything, because you see that *the story isn't real*. Something happened, you had an interpretation about what it meant about you, and you conflated those two things into a fixed truth. In reality, life is totally malleable, and so are you. It's not a fixed and forever truth that you're weird, alone, unwanted, not enough, or whatever other belief you've been living.

In April's case, her mom didn't pick her up that day—that's actually all that happened. But this girl condemned herself to being someone who is alone and not wanted. She made it mean all this stuff about her mom and her world, and then most likely continued to find herself in situations that prove her right.

୬

Author don Miguel Ruiz says that we're all living out a story in which we're the main character, and we cast others to support its validity. Think about it: have you ever known people who are always the victim, and every story they tell is about how they've been wronged, conned, or taken advantage of? Well, that's their role, and they enlist those around them to keep the play running.

When it comes to shaping your own reality, you are incredibly powerful. You create yourself, and that then creates a whole reality (please understand that I am not referring to the true you, but the "not you"—the you that you think of as being who you are). It all just happens unconsciously, as if it's an automatic inheritance. But what you want to get to is that it's all a lie. It's something you made up in reaction to something else that happened, and then you go out and build a whole life based on a lie that over time gets reinforced as true.

You're not a little kid anymore, though, and you can look at all this through mature eyes. You can take responsibility for your way of being in the world.

This practice is about bringing your central lie into view and understanding that *you* did this to yourself—no one else did it. You made a judgment, and *boom!* you got stuck with it. Only you were the one who did the judging and sentencing. Others may have said or implied, "You're stupid," "You can't do that," or whatever else it was, but you accepted it, believed it, and took it on as true. You said it was so. And ever since, you've been living out of that, even though it doesn't serve you.

When you really get that you did this, you can start to own it, give it up, and break free of its hold over you. You see its cost and impact and move from "This is how I was being" to "This is now who I am and what I am committed to being." You can take responsibility for who you've been, how that's impacted every area of your life, and how you now will be.

Creating Fix-Its

As we explored in "Practice #2: Release the Concern for Looking Good," one way to fix a disempowering self-belief that doesn't work is to create a cover-up. We all do that—it's how we survive. We conform or we rebel, but either way it's a reaction to feeling not enough as we are. We think we're not smart enough, so we go out and get five degrees to compensate. Or maybe we don't work to improve our book smarts, but we get focused on doing things right and never taking the risk of looking stupid. We think we're not attractive enough, so we do all kinds of things to make us either conform to or rebel against how we *should* look. We feel alone, so we prove over and over how we don't need anyone, get righteous about how independent we are, become needy for people to like us, or are hopelessly addicted to anyone who will settle for us. But this is the stuff of pretense. It doesn't touch the lie underneath, which is, unbeknownst to our conscious mind, driving the ship.

Consider Joe, who was the youngest of ten kids in a hectic household with busy, overwhelmed parents. As a result of his experiences, his lie was: *I'm not important.* And ever since, he's done everything to prove to himself and the world that he's important. Here's how he explained it:

"My whole life I've been driven by *I'm not important.* I hadn't gotten to those exact words before now—I had other ways of explaining it before—but now I see how *I'm not important* fits with everything. Because I wasn't important to my family, I wasn't important in school, so I studied like crazy to get straight A's. I'm not important at my job, so I work nonstop to keep getting promotions. I'm not important enough to my wife, so everything I do is to get her to acknowledge that I matter to her. Even now, I'm into yoga and spirituality, because in some way it makes me important, maybe even superior. It's like, 'Look at me—I'm conscious, I don't eat meat, I drive an old car, and I'm saving the world.'"

We can actually develop many great skills by being driven by our fix-its. Similar to Joe, we get degrees and take positions of leadership, for example. The good news is that we still get to keep all that. We don't have to give up the competencies, skills, charm, acclaim, knowledge, strength, independence, or great body. But now we get to flow from freedom and create our lives from conscious choice rather than an automatic need to hide, please, or impress others. (It's helpful to note that only those who feel as if they're not enough have to go around proving that they are.)

You *are* whole, and there is nothing you need to prove or justify.

Cara told a story at a workshop in Toronto about how she never quite seemed to fit in with her family. She felt alone and weird, so she made her whole identity about "being different." Without realizing it, though, she also made it about being isolated (separate from), and as a result she was always alienated at school, at work, socially, and even in intimate relationships. I pointed out to Cara that there may be aspects to being different that are cool and could continue to work for her—those that cause her to enjoy being unique—while there also might be aspects that are relegating her to being "apart from" that she may want to drop to gain greater connectedness with others. By giving up the lie that she doesn't belong, she can be authentically unique and actually connect to others through that uniqueness. It's no longer just a knee-jerk reaction to feeling "weird."

If your story doesn't empower you, you have the ability to give it up and come back to samadhi. A clean slate may not be easy, but it's always possible. If you're in a disempowering situation, it's just going to keep showing up, even if you try all kinds of fix-its and strategies so that it doesn't. Whether you move cities, states, relationships, or jobs, that story is always right there waiting to show up because it's the common denominator. It will keep repeating itself until you recognize it as the brick you need to give up, again and again, until it eventually fades away.

Shifting into a New Way of Being

Begin to defy the lie by bringing the defining story out of the shadows and into plain sight. As I say this, perhaps you're already flashing to yours, or at least have a sense of it. It exists in the area of your life where you're disempowered and joyless, where you've resigned yourself to, *This is just how it is.* You don't need to look far and wide for the story's impact; it's actually right in front of you, in the obviousness of your everyday circumstances.

If you say that you don't know what the root story is, you do . . . you just have to really want to see it. It can be something mundane, like your parents telling you to stay away from the crib because you'll hurt your baby brother, a teacher yelling at you for something you didn't do, or a kid making a passing comment that led you to make a judgment about yourself. Unearthing this story and bringing it into view is the first essential step to letting it go.

The second essential step in defying your lie is declaring a new *way of being.* In my trainings, I often tell participants that if they want to be inspiring leaders or teachers, it's not about learning techniques or convincing someone of something. Instead, it's about who they are and letting inspiration come from that. Your genius will come from tapping into a brilliant way of being, where your perspective, thoughts, feelings, and actions are all consistent with what glows genuinely and brightly in your heart.

Earlier we talked about the power of declaration. Declaration is a sacred form of self-expression that uses language to initiate change and transform intention into reality. This isn't about setting goals or objectives; it's something more personal, from your essence and of the heart.

When you're stuck inside your limiting point of view, you don't experience it as a lie. You experience it as the truth, and its rigidity constrains you to only what the present tells you is possible. That's why it's so important to use the power of declaration to separate out the real you from the lie. When you take a stand and declare a new way of being, you open a portal to a new pathway of possibility. And then from there you'll begin living into that possibility. You'll be walking the talk, so to speak.

‿

In Baptiste programs, we do an exercise that centers on the practice of a particular type of declaration that has the power to re-create who you are for yourself and for others. This is an opportunity to use language to create clarity and an authentic foundation from which to move forward.

Begin by locating an area of your life where you want a breakthrough, and then get clear on whatever new way of being you want to embody. It's the true north in your heart. The "languaging" is a key component here, since there's a difference between "being something" and a "way of being." Being something is a layer, or something you put on; being *of* something comes from the depth of your essence. So you want your new way of being to be "*of* a way," "from a space *of*," or "a new world *of*."

For instance:

- "My new way of being is *of* power."
- "My new way of being is *of* love."
- "My new way of being is *of* possibility."
- "My new way of being is *of* courage."
- "My new way of being is *of* connection."
- "My new way of being is *of* lightness."
- "My new way of being is *of* yes."
- "My new way of being is *of* adventure."
- "My new way of being is *of* compassion."

Your declaration is a commitment to the realization of your intention into reality. Next, create "I am . . ." and "I am not . . ." statements that openly defy your lie. The sentences will be preceded by the words, "The lie I am giving up is . . ."

For example:

- "The lie I am giving up is that I am stupid and not worthy."
- "The lie I am giving up is that I am alone and not lovable."
- "The lie I am giving up is that I am fragile and not safe."
- "The lie I am giving up is that I am ugly and not wanted."
- "The lie I am giving up is that I am pathetic and not capable."
- "The lie I am giving up is that I am abandoned and not deserving."

Now, first in writing and then out loud, put the whole statement together, ending with a powerfully declarative, "And *this* is what I am committed to!" So it would look something like this:

> "Right now, my new way of being is of transparency and courage. The lie I am giving up is that I am weak and undeserving. And *this* is what I am committed to!"

I wish I could accurately describe for you the physical and energetic transformation that comes over workshop participants when they stand up with intentionality and make these declarations. It's as though you can see the bricks falling away right in front of your eyes. Doing it causes a huge shift in body language: they stand taller, their energy is lighter and more expansive, and they have a brightness in their eyes that shines from a source deep within.

Like I said before, you don't even have to believe what you're declaring. That's not what this is about. Whether you believe it or not is irrelevant. It's like gravity; you don't have to believe in it, but does that mean it doesn't exist? It's not opinion; practicing these spiritual principles produces actual results.

As you stand in your new way of being and act from it, you'll start getting outside confirmation that the new you is real; that's when the inner liar begins to lose its grip. You start being the change you want to create, and the world starts supporting you as that person. You show up as courageous, and the people around you start seeing you that way. In a sense, you're training your environment to relate to you differently. The bigger you that lives from the heart starts getting stronger and stronger, until it's not even a question of whether you believe your declaration, because it's so present and evident.

When your heart and commitments are aligned, opportunities open up like doors. You'll be able to see and choose what clearly fits your commitments and say no to what doesn't serve your highest intentions. Because you're a yes deep in your being—that's the energy you radiate—the universe just keeps on delivering as you become a beacon for great attractions. You'll start seeing ways to carve out your new path all around you.

As you live out your declaration, it will actually come true, the way it did for my student Amrit. His new way of being was of expansion and exploration, and within three months of making his statement of being and then living from it, he had a job in a different country and a new relationship with someone who he said greatly broadened his horizons.

By the way, in case you need proof that intentionality works, just think about how masterfully you created the *negative* reality that your lie has been dictating all these years. If you believed and declared (even in your head) that you were bad with money, I'm guessing your bank account isn't all that healthy. If you saw yourself as unlovable, chances are that you aren't in the kind of relationship where you feel loved or that you want to be in, if you're in one at all. Yes, you really are so powerful that you brought all this evidence into creation just to prove that you're right.

You want to get really present here to the power of your word, which creates your reality, for better or worse. You say things in a certain way, and then they show up exactly as you intended; what you repeatedly say to yourself each day becomes how it is. Getting intentional with your word empowers you to land in a fresh realm of possibilities.

Sharing your sacred new commitments makes them more and more real in the world. I do, however, want you to consider one pitfall that I've learned on my own path. Nothing kills transformation and sabotages possibility faster than *lip service*. Lip service is a commitment made while standing next to the exit door. Unlike the intentionality of declaration, lip service represents an empty step forward and typically shows up in the form of, "I'll try." It's actually the language of those who are being a no (or even a maybe) in the face of possibility and opportunity but still want to look good. They say, "I'll think about it, and I'll do the best I can." It may not be a final no, but there is no commitment and certainly no power in that kind of expression.

Turning Insight into Action

Remember, this isn't magic. There's work involved. The lie is stubborn, and it doesn't easily dissolve. Almost as quickly as you declare it gone, it might show up again, fighting to stay alive. This is a practice of continually dropping that brick over and over—*through action*.

In yogic principles, there is something called *suka,* which loosely translates to "good space." Suka, in this case, is your insight and intention toward a new way of being. But that alone isn't enough; you also need its balancing principle, *stira,* which means "firm footed and in action." In a yoga pose, having the concept of what you want your body and breath to do is great, but it's not enough. Concepts don't amount to much in reality. You need to move toward that vision with your whole body—muscles, bones, breath, and all.

Insights, "aha!" moments, or even breakthroughs and epiphanies, make no difference in and of themselves, as they quickly become more knowledge, concepts, and theories. It's embodying them and putting them into action that brings about real transformation. In each moment, you're either being intentional (living and creating from your new way of being) or going on automatic response (operating from your lie). The key here is choosing, moment by moment, to live deliberately instead of going on autopilot.

The moment we declare a new way of being, we're presented with opportunities to practice it everywhere and with everyone. I'll always remember Jennifer, a participant at a Journey into Power Bootcamp in Montana. Her new way of being was of community, and she was giving up the lie that she was alone in her life. As soon as we ended the declaring exercise, the whole group walked back from the main hall where we were gathered. It was a very dark night, and the retreat center was up in the mountains, so we needed flashlights to find our way to the cabins. About halfway back, Jennifer realized that she'd forgotten her journal, so she went back to the main hall. As she was walking, the batteries in her flashlight went dead, which left her standing alone and terrified in the pitch-black night, picturing all the wild animals lurking in the woods. Immediately, she went to, "I'm all alone. I'm stranded."

But no, Jennifer was not stranded. She got present and snapped out of the disempowering conversation in her head. Remembering her declaration of being of community, she reached out. She simply said into the darkness, "Hello? Is there anyone nearby?" And sure enough, one of the instructors happened to be around the corner gathering up the day's equipment, and she heard Jennifer and came to help her back to her cabin.

Regardless, Jennifer would have been okay, but the statement she'd just made empowered her, where her old self would have left her feeling diminished. This story is a simple example, sure, but it shows us how quickly the lie can take us out and how, just as quickly, our new way can become reality by turning insight into action. We cement our declarations through action. Shifting our vision isn't enough to make it stick, because how we've done things up to this point will remain powerfully persistent. We must continually act from our new way of being. It's like seeing a $100 bill floating through the air. We can just sit there and ponder it going by, or we could recognize an opportunity and grab it—which is the type of action that turns possibility into reality.

It's funny how this is often where people get tripped up. If we just sit there our whole lives, I can promise that the IRS will eventually come in and take everything. We must continually and actively create our way of being. Otherwise, by default the past stories will flood back in and overpower us. We move forward by taking action and walking through the open doors of life. Amrit's new way of being would have produced no results if he hadn't said yes to the opportunities that were showing up in front of him. Even nonaction is action, as in not reacting as we might have in our old way of being. We must just keep taking the physical steps on our path, whatever they may be.

Every time the lie comes up, move it aside, observe it, give it up, and replace it with the new declaration: "No, that's the lie I give up, not who I am. Who I am is of _____." A new way of being inspires new actions, which then create expanded results. The more times you defy the lie, the weaker it gets, until eventually it fades away entirely.

Will you forget, drop the ball, return to your old way of being, and still live from your lie sometimes? Yes, of course. That's part of being human. The path of transformation isn't linear or final. It's a continual, lifelong process. What matters here is that you live this as an ongoing practice: an untruth shows up, and then you acknowledge it, give it up, make your declaration, and come back to your new way of being. Eventually, you create new musculature—a spiritual one that's stronger than anything you can imagine. So the minute you realize that you've dropped the ball, simply pick it back up—without judgment—and remember that it's yet another awakening, another chance to defy the lie and come into your authentic, empowering way of being.

———— ✑ ————

PRACTICE #9

SET YOUR SIGHTS ON YOUR NORTH STAR

"Make of yourself a light."

— BUDDHA

The path of transformation has no end. It's a profound, lifelong commitment to moving up to something bigger, living in an evolving inquiry, asking with each new insight what's possible, and loving the possibility of growing beyond who you know yourself to be.

Much of what you've put into practice here is about what I call true-north alignment. This is where we bring it all together into aligning ourselves always, in all ways, into whole-life integration. Gandhi said, "Happiness is when what you think, what you say, and what you do are in harmony." That is integration. Taking your personal philosophy out of the mental ashram and putting it into practice in your everyday world makes it real and alive.

You have a North Star that illuminates your path to an extraordinary existence. I don't literally mean a star, of course, but symbolically and energetically—a spiritual focal point that is within you, beyond you, and leads you toward something greater. It's the bright future that you are living now. Your North Star empowers and informs your actions in this moment. It gives you your thoughts, attitudes, point of view, and body sensations in the present. In Eastern spiritual principles, acting toward that greater purpose is referred to as *sadhana,* which means that you're being intentional in life, staying true to creating continual aliveness and expressing it through your everyday activities and commitments.

As you put the practice of aligning to your North Star into action, you will do a lot of great clearing. You're giving up bricks, letting go of old ways of being and seeing, releasing resentments and fears, cleaning up past messes, forgiving yourself and others, and dropping disempowering stories. The universe will not tolerate empty space, though, so if you're not consciously filling it with new, positive actions and energy, what will? The past, by default. This is the idea of sadhana practice: intentionally filling the space. If we don't do this, then the habitual patterns of old start to take over again, and we get more of the same.

Maybe you weren't purposefully creating into your space in the past. Maybe you were unconsciously and reactively filling it with drama, cynicism, resignation, and so on. Pause for a moment, and examine your life up until now. How has it turned out? Another way to say that is, "How have you been filling your space?" What you see before you and around you is a direct result of how and who you've been. It's not a question of the right or wrong reality, but whether it's working for you. Does it need updating and new energy? What's next?

Sometimes people share with me that they haven't been inspired about anything in their lives for years. That can be difficult to confront for many individuals, but they can allow feedback to be the fuel that motivates them to create a new reality. You can commit to sadhana and make what you want real. By putting into action the nine practices for igniting your life, you bring forth the possibility of creating yourself and your life as a true expression of who you are. These practices don't necessarily enhance or improve the options you have in front of you; rather, what you're given in each moment is the power to choose who you'll be and how you'll fill your space and your future.

Creating Tadasana

In yoga asana practice, *Tadasana,* also known as Mountain Pose, is the true north of all yoga poses, because it allows you to tune in to your body and hold it as a clearing for possibility. In this pose, you stand upright with a sense of vitality, your feet grounded and activated a few inches apart. Your spine is stacked, relaxed, and straight; your arms are extended by your sides; and all your muscles are drawing in toward your centerline and core so that all parts of your body integrate and work together in harmony as if they were notes in an orchestral arrangement. Your eyes are focused forward with a calm determination. Much like a ballerina performing on a stage, the pose appears effortless yet dynamic.

Anyone walking by a yoga class on any given day might look in and see students in Tadasana and think they're pretty much just standing there, which, on one level, they are. But on a whole other level, they're putting into action the physical and energetic practices that create the foundation of all asana practice, because every pose begins with that sense of inner alignment—it empowers students to move and breathe from their center.

Lose Tadasana, your true north, and you lose your power and what's possible in the pose. When you find that you're off center, restore integrity by coming back to true north alignment of Tadasana and begin again. The same holds true in your spiritual life. That energetic center is where you access your power.

There will be lots of times where you'll feel that sense of whole-body, life alignment. Things will be expanding and flowing, and you'll feel open, vital, and creative . . . all the energetic results of being in and of your power. You'll feel it one day, and the next you might find yourself struggling again, wondering where it went. But remember, there is nothing to fix. There is nothing wrong with exactly *what is so,* as it is. In these moments, you want to simply get present to where you are and ask that one simple question: "What do I need to give up right now in order to be at peace?"

You may fall back—sometimes even three, four, or five steps. When you do, just pick yourself up, dust yourself off, restore true north, and find Tadasana again. No drama, no story. When we're committed to something bigger, it doesn't mean that we won't have failures or setbacks. It just means that we don't quit when we do. As Lao-tzu said, "Life is not about never falling, but rather it's about getting up each time we fall."

It's a constant practice. In each moment that you wake up and realize you've lost Tadasana, turn that insight into action, recommit, and begin again. The spiritual muscle you are creating is getting stronger right now, and, as with any muscle, it needs repetition to continue to build. Over and over, it's a realization of, "Wait. This is old, unconscious stuff. I know what it costs me, and I'm not going back into that box. The lid is going to stay on this time."

Standing in Tadasana is immediately grounding and gives you access to a solid foundation. Consider that whenever anything upsets you, you're in your thoughts and not present, and when that's the case, outside forces can get to you and knock you off balance. You're "messable" anytime you feel threatened by a situation, and this is a big clue that you're not operating from your true north.

I've had the privilege of co-creating and being involved in the Africa Yoga Project with Paige Elenson, one of my longtime friends and students. I've visited Kenya several times to teach yoga to some of the most impoverished but spiritually hungry and alive individuals I've ever met. At the same time, these people are living with centuries of political and social unrest, which I experienced on my last visit.

At one of the leadership sessions, there was a kirtan master who was leading the participants in a chant to the Indian deity Ganesha. This was a group that represented different tribes and religions, some of whom were devout Muslims who did not take the least bit kindly to anything related to Hinduism, and all hell broke loose. Some of the students flew into a rage, ready to battle the yogis who embraced the Hindu references. The chaos and fury I had to navigate that day were amazing—this was unlike anything I'd done as a teacher up to that point in my life.

When I finally got the room calmed down, I turned to the man—a Muslim—who had been ready to physically fight one of the other participants and calmly asked him, "Why are you threatened? Why do you need to take him down in order to be right? If you have your god, why are you threatened by his?" What emerged was a dynamic conversation and inquiry into the idea of being "messable," which brought the whole group into a space of greater acceptance.

When you're flowing from your center, other people's judgments or opinions can't stir you up. You're on purpose with your eyes set on the prize, and what they say, believe, or do doesn't easily stir you up, trigger you, or stop you from being yourself. I'm not talking about pretending something doesn't bother you; remember, at the heart of all of this is authenticity. I'm talking about putting into practice the tool of not having to make someone else wrong in order to be able to stand in your own truth. There is your truth, their truth, and probably 100 other truths in between. None are wrong, and none are right. They just *are*. Let them be. So what if someone feels differently than you do? What does it cost you to let them be right? Nothing. What does it cost you to make them wrong? Your peace of mind, your energy for what you really want to create in your life, your power. . . . The choice is yours.

Wherever you are in your life, you want to find the inner stillness of Tadasana. When sailors are out at sea and they hit a storm, their strategy is to go straight into the eye of it and hang out in that stillness as the storm rages around them. Well, circumstances may be raging around you, but your work here is to use the transformational tools to stay true to what you are committed to and find your way to the calm center of spiritual power that's always available within.

Your North-Star Principles

In "Practice #8: Defy the Lie," I talked about how insights mean nothing without action, and this is especially relevant as you set about creating a life that reflects what's most important to your heart.

Commitment is a technique I personally use to get clarity and intentionality for a vision of my life. The guiding values and practices that I'm operating from are a pathway to shape my vision. This vision is my North Star, and defining, writing down, and revisiting these practices is another way for me to stay connected to true north.

I'd like you to create your true north now with this process. You'll want to spend 20 minutes or so writing in a journal the qualities you most value, such as authenticity, connection, love, truth, power, peace, vitality, or freedom, just to name a few. Write about how and why these are foundational to how you're choosing to live. Imagine various situations in which these North-Star principles can be a part of your life (or be challenged) and what they would look like if they were. Then set a clear intention and commit to living to what you wrote.

Every morning and every night, shortly after you awaken and right before you go to sleep, review your list. Reviewing it twice each day gives you two solid opportunities to notice where you are and how you're doing. This empowering exercise will support keeping you aligned and connected to these principles, and also give you feedback about where you might have veered off course. As with anyone walking a path, you need to make sure you stay on course, as there will be milestones and measures that will reflect your journey.

If you fall out of integrity, please give up the temptation to go into story land and make it mean something! Just find your footing and root down into Tadasana, again and again. Recommit to your North Star, and move forward with renewed integrity and intentionality. In moments of emotional upset, you want to quickly revert to thinking that this too shall pass. Upset is akin to emotional indigestion—just try to let it go and get back to what you were up to before the situation occurred.

Another technique that's amazingly effective for whole-life mastery is a visioning exercise. For this one, you'll want to take out your journal and write the following:

By the end of _____ [insert date here for accountability], *I will . . .*

- ◆   *. . . expand the boundaries of* _____.

- ◆   *. . . establish new playgrounds of possibility in* _____.

- ◆   *. . . invite surprise and adventure in* _____.

- ◆   *. . . be one of life's players in* _____.

- ◆   *. . . disrupt business as usual and affirm creation in* _____.

Be very thoughtful about what you write down and wish for, because remember, there is huge power in putting this out there! Every person I've heard back from who has fully taken on this exercise tells me that nearly all of these visions became reality once they began living from their power.

Finding Your True Purpose and Passion

Earlier in the book, I mentioned a point in my life when I felt really lost. I was in my early 20s and had just moved to L.A. I didn't know where I was going, and I didn't know who I was. Spiritually speaking, I was seeking, but I felt confused. I was doing yoga and meditating, and I'd pray, *Guide me. Show me where to go, what to do.* Even so, I wasn't evolving or changing in the way I really needed. I was stuck, big time.

I eventually found a meditation teacher who inspired me. Something about what he was saying and teaching moved me and tapped into some kind of truth within me. I went to him and said, "You know, I'm totally lost and confused about what I'm supposed to be doing in my life."

He replied, "Well, you don't have love."

I kind of didn't really get that at first. I mean, I could get it on a bumper-sticker level, but it wasn't resonating with anything deeper in me.

He could tell, so he put it another way. "You don't have purpose, and purpose is love," he explained. "A purpose that's bigger than who you are and that you expand into allows for the presence of love."

It wasn't as if I magically found my purpose in that moment, but his words hit home. It was a pivotal step for me to see that I needed to create space for bigger possibilities and a purpose. I didn't know what that was yet, so I just let the not knowing be. I trusted that I was on the path for it to eventually be revealed to me. From that day on, my outlook was more specific. It was like this: *I don't want to waste time and play disempowering games anymore. What is my true purpose?* Creating this particular space and way of being, which unexpectedly allowed for the possibility of my life to truly make a difference, was an empowering context for me.

I shifted my perception from acquiring more strategies and skills to exploring and authentically engaging with questions such as, *What is my life really going to be about? What does it mean to be human?* and *What matters most?* I was open to a breakthrough, and I started to put my attention on what gave me that spark of inspiration in my heart—which, of course, was making a difference on the planet, teaching power yoga, and inspiring others.

We all have that little charge of energy around those things that we connect with; that's where the opportunity is for purpose and the new possibility of love. For a lot of yoga instructors, that's why they show up to teach. They have a passion to inspire others and share what they've gotten from their practice. And then they see that it's an actual opportunity to keep growing and expanding themselves. (By the way, this doesn't mean that once you find your energetic purpose everything becomes easy. Remember, everyone faces obstacles. That's where setting your sights to your North Star will get you through.)

Eventually, I began teaching yoga full-time, and my whole world opened up. It was a true expression of the heart for me. My love for the practice and my passion for sharing it lit me up. I had a vision for how to simplify yoga and present it in a way that people from all walks of life could understand and use to transform their lives, so that's the direction I went in.

But back then, when I was a young teacher with a new house and a family to feed, I had many sleepless nights, especially when we were running low on money.

We often struggled to make ends meet, and keeping my dream alive was very tough. In fact, it was one of the hardest things I've ever done, because the need to stay financially afloat brought up a lot of fear. Then I went through a painful divorce and the experience of having two business partnerships fall through, back to back. Although much of this was confronting on many levels, never once did I let go of my vision, and I learned hugely valuable life lessons as a result.

A major one I learned is that I was 100 percent responsible—yes, 100 percent—for how life showed up for me. I sourced all of it. I saw that many of the relationships I considered failures were actually successful graduations to becoming more authentic! Consider this idea: life is an educational adventure—the highs, lows, and everything in between.

I've taught and worked closely with many individuals who are very successful in different industries, including music, sports, film, politics, the ministry, and the field of human development. What many of them don't talk about is the pain that is likely to be felt when someone falls short of their vision. We might get the impression that these individuals' careers were magnificent, brilliant, and smooth from the start, but of course, nothing could be farther from the truth. Often the barriers to realizing our aspirations are a lot of very unhappy things. They're those issues that few people talk about, because not many of us are willing to confront these things in ourselves.

Your greatest tests will come in the dark moments when your soul is being squeezed. That's when you want to be grounded in your bigger purpose—your North Star. When your heart is truly lit up about something, you don't do it, it does you, and perseverance becomes the only choice. Being resilient allows you to break through to what's next when you're challenged with obstacles in your path. Aligned to the power of love in your heart, you will be a gift to yourself and others. Rather than sparring with what's confronting you, you'll be creating space for grace.

In life, we must all sometimes know pain, but we also need to be fully aware of the ways we disempower ourselves by undermining or sabotaging the process of transforming our intentions into reality. At the end of the day, we either have the results we want (our intentions made real), or we have the reasons, stories, and justifications for why we don't. The person who's being of power doesn't dwell in explanations and excuses, but rather in what's happening in reality and the realization of conscious results.

The Greatest Calling

I'd just completed a workshop in Denver, when a student approached me saying that he wanted to share an important revelation with me. He told me that while we were meditating, he discovered that he was God—that they were one. He was clear as a bell about his realization, and my sense was that he wanted me to rejoice with him in his discovery.

I looked at him and said, "Okay, that's really good. Now I want you to go to Darfur and feed the hungry and straighten out the situation there."

The color left his face, and I could tell he was angry. It was obvious that he'd wanted my admiration for his breakthrough. We talked for a few minutes more, and I explained that although it was a cool and empowering discovery, his own transformation unshared was worthless. If he wanted to truly embody godliness, then his next natural steps would be to create results for other people.

The true secret of a great life, as I see it, is making a difference for others. All else is empty. When we're empowering others through our sharing, that's when we get what we really, really want. If we love something that's bigger than we are, we're in service to something that uses and possesses us. It's so inspiring, that it's natural to want to share it. And then, we find that what we give to others ends up expanding and manifesting even more within ourselves. Inspiration stimulates generosity, which in turn inspires, and on and on the cycle goes.

For most of us, life has been oriented around me, myself, and I. But at a certain point, that creates only emptiness. From there, we can easily end up medicated, physically exhausted or ill, depressed, or just plain unhappy. The key here is to look at the energy we're exchanging with other human beings.

∽

One of the Ten Commandments is about not stealing, and that goes beyond just material goods. There's also the stealing of other people's energy. Have you ever heard of *psychic vampirism?* Well, there are certain individuals who can suck out all your energy when you're around them. For example, you spend an hour with them and feel exhausted and drained when you leave. Do you know anyone like that?

In life, you can either be an energy sucker or an energy creator. Are you someone who's draining, or do you leave other people inspired? Consider who you are in relation to others' life force. When you're inauthentic, it's inherent that you won't create energy; there's no light in your eyes. But when you're in your power, there's a kind of charisma. You walk into a room and the lights get brighter, people sit up a little straighter, and energy gets generated. That's called *asteya*—being someone who generates life.

Albert Schweitzer said, "I don't know what your destiny will be. But one thing I know: The only ones among you who will be really happy are those who have sought and found how to serve." Note that he didn't say "try to serve." Fulfillment, happiness, and real power come from having served fully, and in such a way where you continue to expand in your own ability to love, contribute, and make a difference.

Which kind of person are you evolving to be—an energy taker or energy creator?

The Power of Sharing

When you share your love with another person, it isn't depleted or diminished; rather, it expands. The same is true with using the nine practices in this book. The more you talk about your experiences, the deeper they'll become. Insights, inspiration, and new ideas that are released into the universe will spread and grow. The practice of offering what you're accomplishing in your transformational practice is yet another source of power.

An important aspect of essential speaking in the realm of growth is to simply share your experience. What impact are the practices having on you? What do you see about yourself or your life that you didn't before, and what's now available for you?

Sometimes we don't share what's important to us so as to not lose any of it, but we'll soon see that the more we do offer our experiences and commitments to others, the more energy builds around them, and the more we'll experience opportunities opening up.

When you make things happen for yourself and tell the world about it, your environment is elevated. Expressing yourself creatively may light the fire that others need to do something for themselves. By your sharing in word and action, some people will start to take on what you're up to; before you know it, a community is formed where everyone is exploring, learning, and working together to support you in whatever you're up to.

AFTERWORD

It is my greatest hope that the practices you've found here awaken the magnificent power within you that has been there all along. May they inspire you to attract and create all the miracles that you're capable of and more.

We all have an opportunity to shine and be an example in our own unique way. This planet needs you. Yes, *you*. This is your life right here . . . this is it. Let today, in each new moment, be about stepping up and filling the space in your heart, life, and world with radiance and a power sourced from love. Let today be about walking in awareness and taking actions from the space that allows us to breakthrough and play bigger than we ever imagined, even in the smallest of things.

George Bernard Shaw said something that basically sums up a sense I have about what ultimately gives real power. He said, "This is the true joy in life—that being used for a purpose recognized by yourself as a mighty one." It will require courage, boldness, and heart. More radical than any revolution is the evolution of one's self and making a powerful difference by expanding your brilliance out to all, one human being at a time.

Aligning to the divine is always available to you at any moment. Invite in those highest intentions for this day, this experience, this life. Act on those intentions, and transform them into reality. From this space, where you are right here, right now, ask of the highest good, because it's yours to request. You, the authentic, true you, are of a divine power.

By transforming from within, you'll have awakened the greatest power of all: the power to transform the world.

If not you, who?

If not here, where?

And if not now, when?

I wish you joy, love, and great expansion on your journey.

———— ✌ ————

ACKNOWLEDGMENTS

I have been a speaker, teacher, and social visionary in the realm of personal development and yoga for 30 years. I've had the good fortune to travel and visit with remarkable people all over the planet, and over and over again I'm always struck by the realization that when it comes to making a difference with what matters most in our humanity, no one does anything alone.

This book is no exception. I'm grateful to all of the extraordinary people who made this journey possible for me. There's no such thing as a book separate from all the people and experiences that gave shape and influence to the life and thinking of the author, and this stands very true for me.

I acknowledge the teachers who have been a source of power on my journey. I've learned that those who have blessed me need to be the first for me to bless and recognize out loud. I have infinite gratitude to all those whose life and work have powerfully impacted my perceptions, my life, and my leading of this work, especially Walt and Magaña Baptiste, B.K.S. Iyengar, Krishnamacharya, and Bikram Choudhury for their emphasis on the discipline and power of using physical yoga practices to transform one's experience of the world and apply it in his or her life.

I have enormous appreciation for Roy Masters and S. N. Goenka for guiding me with compassion and unapologetic rigor through the practice of meditation, which ultimately gave me access to an embodied learning and the living out of the practices in this book.

John Bradshaw, Fernando Flores, former NFL coach John Gruden, Landmark Education, Peter Block, Ron Bynum, Chip Wilson, Susanne Conrad, Jenna Buffaloe, and Kip Flock—the thoughts and sentences I speak and write have all been shaped by their contribution in some way. I don't know if I have a thought or idea that is truly and originally my own, so I happily take my seat as a secondary source for some aspects of their work where my own transformation was expanded. Due to them, I live with a spark of possibility and engaged in an expansive future.

I deeply appreciate the many, many people who have participated in Baptiste training programs, workshops, and classes and made this work a part of their transformational journey. Your commitment, questions, challenges, insights, input, and breakthroughs have elevated me and taught me to appreciate what it is to be fully human.

This book exists as a result of the enthusiastic urging of my publisher, Hay House: Louise Hay, Reid Tracy, and their amazing team. Hay House is a publishing company that lives out the empowering ideas contained in what it publishes. I am grateful to Reid Tracy, who has been a patient and supportive guide for the focus of this book very early on in its formation and through its various re-creations.

I thank Debra Goldstein, my all-time favorite writer and wordsmith of choice, for her dedication to impeccability. Her commitment to excellence was demonstrated over and over as she worked to organize, generate, and give shape to the manuscript through many iterations of my writing. Debra is a master of her craft, and I am grateful for our working partnership.

I thank Ned Leavitt, my trusted literary agent, who has depth of heart, intelligence, and wise perspective. I thank Ken Browning, my trusted manager and agent, for always getting it done and empowering the next level of who I am and what I'm up to.

I thank the Baptiste Institute staff, Baptiste Certified teachers, and the Baptiste Affiliated Yoga Schools who dynamically share and practice in this work and methodology.

I thank Mark Aronchick, Jim Meade, David Ruben, and Dr. Ronald Podel for real mentoring at critical points in my life that have contributed very much to my education and depth of experience. I thank Leah Cullis, who supported me on many paths that were timely for me to walk. I thank Amelia Gailey for her support and for being herself.

I thank my parents for gifting me with a presence on this earth. All my blessings are a reflection of their love for one another and for me. I love you both forever.

To the extent that I got things right, I thank all of these individuals. To the extent I missed the mark—that rests entirely with me.

— **Baron Baptiste**, Park City, Utah, December 2012

—⌀—

ABOUT THE AUTHOR

Baron Baptiste's popularity as an international pre-senter and best-selling author is exemplified by his creation of a wildly popular yoga practice that is a methodology for personal revolution. For 20 years, he has been a dynamic and influential teacher, trainer, leader, and catalyst in the arena of spiritual, physical, and life transformation. His work powerfully creates bridges from the wisdom of the East to the spiritually hungry West.

Baron transformed the training methods of NFL players as a peak-performance specialist on the Philadelphia Eagles coaching staff, and has also taught many Hollywood celeb-rities. He has appeared on thousands of radio and television programs, including the PBS special *Transform Your Life: Yoga with Baron Baptiste.*

NOTES

NOTES

NOTES

NOTES

NOTES

NOTES

NOTES

NOTES

NOTES

NOTES

Hay House Titles of Related Interest

We hope you enjoyed this Hay House book. If you'd
like to receive our online catalog featuring additional
information on Hay House books and products,
or if you'd like to find out more about the
Hay Foundation, please contact:

Hay House, Inc., P.O. Box 5100, Carlsbad, CA 92018-5100
(760) 431-7695 or (800) 654-5126
(760) 431-6948 (fax) or (800) 650-5115 (fax)
www.hayhouse.com® • **www.hayfoundation.org**

ᔕ

Published and distributed in Australia by: Hay House Australia Pty.
Ltd., 18/36 Ralph St., Alexandria NSW 2015 • *Phone:* 612-9669-4299
Fax: 612-9669-4144 • www.hayhouse.com.au

Published and distributed in the United Kingdom by: Hay House
UK, Ltd., Astley House, 33 Notting Hill Gate, London W11 3JQ • *Phone:*
44-20-3675-2450 • *Fax:* 44-20-3675-2451 • www.hayhouse.co.uk

Published and distributed in the Republic of South Africa by:
Hay House SA (Pty), Ltd., P.O. Box 990, Witkoppen 2068
Phone/Fax: 27-11-467-8904 • www.hayhouse.co.za

Published in India by: Hay House Publishers India, Muskaan
Complex, Plot No. 3, B-2, Vasant Kunj, New Delhi 110 070
Phone: 91-11-4176-1620 • *Fax:* 91-11-4176-1630 • www.hayhouse.co.in

Distributed in Canada by: Raincoast, 9050 Shaughnessy St.,
Vancouver, B.C. V6P 6E5 *Phone:* (604) 323-7100 • *Fax:* (604) 323-2600
www.raincoast.com

ᔕ

Take Your Soul on a Vacation

Visit **www.HealYourLife.com®** to regroup, recharge,
and reconnect with your own magnificence.
Featuring blogs, mind-body-spirit news, and life-changing
wisdom from Louise Hay and friends.

Visit **www.HealYourLife.com** today!